LET YOUR BODY
INTERPRET YOUR DREAMS

EUGENE T. GENDLIN, Ph.D.
University of Chicago

Author of *Focusing*

CHIRON PUBLICATIONS • Wilmette, Illinois

© 1986 by Chiron Publications. All rights
reserved. No part of this publication may be
reproduced, stored in a retrieval system, or
transmitted, in any form by any means, electronic,
mechanical, photocopying, recording, or otherwise, without the prior written permission of the
publisher, Chiron Publications,
400 Linden Avenue, Wilmette, Illinois 60091.

Printed in the United States of America

Book design by Elaine M. Hill

Library of Congress
Cataloging-in-Publication Data

Gendlin, Eugene T., 1926–
Let your body interpret your dreams.

Bibliography: p.
1. Dreams. 2. Body, Human, I. Title.
BF1078.G395 1986 154,6'34 85-26920
ISBN 0-933029-01-2 (pbk.)

Contents

Chapter 1

Introduction

The method of dream-interpretation presented in this book has three advantages: *First, it is not limited to any one theory or belief system.* The experts give conflicting interpretations. They approach a dream from different angles. Here is a way to use all their approaches without being committed to one of them.

Second, the basic touchstone of the method is your own bodily experience of something opening up in you. An interpretation is sure if, and only if, you have a breakthrough, *a physical felt shift.*

Let me tell you immediately, on the first page of the book, what this touchstone is:

As an example, suppose you have forgotten one of the things you were supposed to do today. You know there was something, but not what it was. You have an odd, unclear sense (we call it a felt sense) of this forgotten task. You try out various ideas, such as, "It must have been something about work," or "Maybe it was that thing Jeannie wanted me to do." These are good ideas. They are things you need to do. But if that unclear sense doesn't budge, you know you have not remembered *the* forgotten task. When at last you do remember, there is a *physically felt* relief, as it all floods back. Whew!!! You remember not only what you were going to do, but also why, where, with whom, and what you feel about it. By then if someone asked you, "How do you know this is what you forgot?" (and not "something about work" and not "Jeannie's thing"), you would laugh. In your body the feeling is unmistakable. You have remembered.

A breakthrough with a dream is like that. Before, the dream seemed crazy, meant nothing, and gave you only a puzzling felt sense. Suddenly it is all about a certain part of your life, and you *know* it. Such a break-

1

through comes with a physically felt release, a bit of energy freed up *in your body*. Before the breakthrough, various ideas could fit the dream. Now there is no question of mere fitting, mere likelihood. You *know* what it is about.

Later we will take up certain subtler bodily responses you can distinguish to work further with a dream.

Third, the method can be taught and learned. I have taken the theories of various experts and turned them into questions. You can ask yourself these questions (or, if you are interpreting someone else's dream, you can ask that person). You ask the questions slowly, one by one, until the felt sense of the dream opens and the breakthrough occurs. Although the experts differ, you can tap the dream with a question from one of them, and then a question from another and another. With different dreams different questions lead to a breakthrough—the felt shift.

The method is "focusing" applied to dreams (Gendlin 1981). A string of research studies has shown that change comes when there is a certain kind of bodily attention we now call focusing (Mathieu-Coughlan and Klein 1984). When change happened, people did not only talk or think. Nor did they only feel the same emotions over and over, however intensely. Rather, they also physically sensed what could not be defined.

One can recognize this way of attending. The person says something. There is a little silence ..... Then the person says: "No, that's not quite right. I feel it right there, but I don't know what it is. Yet I do know that what I just said isn't right. There is another silence ....."

Then suddenly the person says, "Oh, I know! One thing about it is ....." Having said some sentences, the person asks: "Is that right?" Again there is a silence .....

Now the person may say: "No. That isn't right, either."

Or, there may be a breath, the person's posture may ease. "Whew, yes, that's right. Whew. That's it, all right."

The research finds change and problem-resolution predictable for those who attend in this way. Those who only talk, think, or feel recognizable emotions mostly do not change.

That finding has been consistent in many studies.

Most people don't know this odd mode of physical attention. Only at rare times do they physically experience a meaning-sense they cannot grasp. It happens when one has a "hunch." Perhaps some situation, say a job offer, seems excellent. It makes perfect logical sense to say yes. Yet one may have a fuzzy, queasy feeling in one's body about it. One does not know why, and cannot define it, but .....

Such a "felt sense" is rare. But, if you know focusing, you can get a felt sense about any topic, almost any time you want.

We now teach focusing to people in many different contexts. But learning it requires some time and practice. Focusing can be learned by working with dreams. The hardest part is to let a felt sense come. With a dream that is *often* easy. A dream usually brings you a felt sense. *If not, it soon comes if you attend in your body while pondering the dream.* The felt sense is that fuzzy body-sense, that odd, vague quality the dream gives you.

Sometimes you don't remember a dream, but you know you had one. How do you know? You have the felt sense of the dream when you wake up. If you *focus* your attention on this fuzzy sense, tap at it, perhaps lose track, tap at it again, the dream may suddenly come back.

The felt sense is most noticeable when nothing else is left from the dream. But you can have the felt sense along with a remembered dream.

The felt sense isn't a usual feeling, like angry, scared, or sad. In addition to such *recognizable feelings* a dream also leaves you with a unique felt quality that fits no category. You cannot think it. It is an indefinable, global, puzzling, odd, uneasy, *fuzzy sense in your body*.

With our method you direct the questions *there*—to the felt sense. Then you wait to see if something new comes in you.

At first people answer questions about a dream quickly by saying "No. Nothing." "What does the dream remind you of?" "Nothing." "What does that house remind you of?" "Nothing." But each question needs about a minute. Rather than instantly saying, "No, nothing," you sit with it a little. The time is not so long that you get bored or strained but just long enough to let the question touch the felt sense of the dream.

You are not asking your mind the question. You are asking the felt sense of the dream *in your body*.

The traditional way to "interpret" dreams applies one viewpoint and arrives at some conclusions. I deny that dreams can be interpreted that way. Such conclusions are only hypotheses. There is no interpretation until something pops out for the dreamer, concretely and experientially, in response to the hypothesis. Therefore I have turned these different viewpoints into *questions*. You slowly ask the body's felt sense a question. If nothing comes, proceed to another question.

When the felt sense itself answers, there is a physical signal, a tension release, a felt shift. What comes with that is concrete for you—you won't need me to tell you it's genuine and that you are interpreting your dream.

That is our touchstone.

I owe this form of the method to my three visiting years at Richmond College in the City University of New York. The students were largely nurses, housewives, policemen, working people who were trying school.

My task was to formulate things simply and clearly *without losing the essence*. To do that, I had to separate the essence and make it more precise than it was. That produced an advance. I dedicate this book to Richmond College.

The way I found to teach dream-interpretation went somewhat beyond the usual class. Of course we used the books of Freud and Jung in class. But the method of focusing plus questions enabled nearly all the students to interpret their dreams quite concretely and to help other students to grasp theirs. They all went on to do it for spouses and friends. In a certain odd sense, the students were doing more than is common among experts. Even seasoned professionals rarely interpret a dream with experiential corroboration rather than guesswork. I saw that the students and I had developed a new professional method. I was surprised.

The students did not know enough about the field to be surprised. They simply accepted this new power as something one learns in college. But they were certainly enthusiastic. At the end of one course, a student told me, "I can interpret my dreams and get my wife and other people to do it. I worked with the girl next door until she could do it, and it helped her a lot. I'm putting you into my Book of Life because you gave me that." This kind of thing is a teacher's best reward.

The three advantages are: that we can use all the experts together, that the touchstone is always the dreamer's own bodily response, and that the method can be learned.

Now that I have bragged about these innovations, I must also present them more modestly. Nothing we say about human beings is sure. Dreams are mysterious, nothing about them is sure. We have no sure understanding of dreams. What I offer is really a method of modesty. An interpretation from one theory makes a lot of sense, but when you hear the interpretation from another theory, it makes sense too. And there are many theories. It is more modest to stay open to all ways of interpreting. Only what comes freshly in your body interprets your dream.

Even this is only one method. It does not foreclose other possibilities with dreams.

The method is also not quite as simple as I said so far.

The method has a second part.

There are two stages of dream-interpretation. (Sometimes they occur all at once, sometimes not.) A breakthrough may let you know *what the dream is about,* but you may find that it teaches you nothing you didn't know before. Then it was only Stage 1 of dream interpretation. You can go on to a second stage, as I will show—but this does not succeed with every dream. When it does, you get *something new for your own development.*

So the method is a little more complicated than just asking questions until the felt sense of the dream opens. A second stage is usually needed. In the second part we also apply the vital BIAS CONTROL, which I explain in Chapter 10. We need it to move around a pitfall we all face when we interpret *our own* dreams: We tend to put on the dream the same mistaken view we put on anything in life. Then the dream seems to say the sort of thing we always say to ourselves.

My dream is made in my body. You might say it comes from me, but "me" is multiple. The human subjectivity is not a single thing. The usual conscious "me" is many processes, but it constitutes only a small part of what humans may be. You can also say the dream happens to me. (We don't want to stay within any one conception of dreams—or of humans.) At any rate it is more than what I know. But, when I interpret my own dream, I use meanings I know. Therefore I must exactly miss what is more than I already know. How can I get beyond that?

Everyone who studied dreams found this problem. They all concluded that people cannot interpret their own dreams. The BIAS CONTROL solves this puzzle.

How can I get beyond imposing my usual conscious attitudes on the dream? The BIAS CONTROL enables my body to do it, not every time, but often.

When I explain the BIAS CONTROL, you will see exactly how. Here I only alert you to this problem and let you know about the second stage of the method.

Most of what I know about dreams comes from Bonime (1962), Boss (1958), Ernest FitzHugh, Freud, Mary Hendricks, Barbara Ingram, Jung, Malamud (1967, 1979) Perls, Arvind Vasavada, Whitmont (1978), H. R. Wijngaarden, and a brilliant article by Berry (1974). I provided only the new method, the bodily touchstone which lets us use the many approaces in this way. The method comes from focusing (which came from the research and philosophical work on thinking and experiencing).

Focusing seems odd at first. You pay attention to something vague, something you don't recognize! It is definitely there, all right, *this* odd sense, in your body. But you cannot say what it is. At first it seems so vague, hardly worth your attention. "That's nothing," you might say. "What can come from that?" But *that* is how your body has the dream. In that felt sense is everything your organism knows. And more! In *that* is how your organism needs to move, its next growth step. But that step is not fully determined until it comes.

All this cannot be clear right here. Let us take it up slowly.

I

Breakthrough

Chapter 2

The Questions

This chapter introduces the questions. I don't explain them here. I just list them for easy learning and remembering. Each question is explained further in Appendix B. Look there, now or later, for how to use them.

You will never need all the questions with one dream. Only the first one needs to be asked every time. Then scan the list in your mind and choose some question to ask next.

The questions are not addressed to the dreamer. Rather, they are for the dreamer to ask the body. Let the question go on down, inside. Ask it there. It takes about a minute or so per question. Then, if nothing comes, go to another question.

If you are interpreting other people's dreams, make clear that they need not tell you what comes in them. They can keep that to themselves if they wish. Ask the dreamer to indicate when something came. When it does, say: "Stay silently with that for a little while. See where it goes." It helps to give something new a minute or two. Then, if the person wants to, it is all right to say some of it.

Question #1 always comes first because it lets associations come freely. All the other questions can be asked in any order.

1. **WHAT COMES TO YOU?**
   What are your associations in relation to the dream?
   What comes to mind as you think about the dream?
   Or pick a part of the dream. What comes to you in relation to that?

2. **FEELING?**
   What did you feel in the dream?

9

Sense the feel-quality of the dream. Let it come back as fully as possible.

Choose the most puzzling, oddest, most striking, or most beautiful part of the dream. Picture it to yourself and let a felt sense of it come in your body.

Or pick one part of the dream.

Then ask: What in your life feels like that?

Or: What does this feel-quality remind you of? When did you ever feel like that?

Or: What is new for you in that felt sense?

3. YESTERDAY?

What did you do yesterday? Scan your memory of yesterday. Also recall what you were inwardly preoccupied with.

Something related to the dream may come up.

Questions #1, #2, and #3 offer three ways to get associations.

If some associations came, you need not go on and on to get more. You need not ask all three questions. You can come back to them later in relation to any part of the dream.

4. PLACE?

Visualize and sense the lay-out of the main place in your dream.

What does it remind you of?

Where have you been in a place like that?

What place felt like that?

5. STORY?

First summarize the story-plot of the dream. Then ask yourself: What in your life is like that story?

Summarize the events of the dream in two or three steps: "first . . .and then . . .and then. . ." Make it more general than the dream. This can be done in several ways, if the first way has no effect.

Example: Crossing the River Dream

I had to cross this river, there was no way across, then I saw a bridge further down but when I got there it was only to an island in the river.

The story-summary might be: "First there seems to be no way, then there is one, but only part way. What in your life is like that?"

Or: "First you're discouraged, then it's better but not all O.K. What in your life is like that?"

Or: "First it's one big gap across. Then it turns out there is a place in between."

Story plot summaries let you ask: What is like that for you? Where in your life are you now lacking a way? What are you discouraged about? What seems like one big gap, all or nothing, right now? What might be like that island?

6. CHARACTERS?

Take the unknown person in your dream. Or, if you know them all, take the most important. (Or take them up in turn.)

What does this person remind you of? What physical feel-quality does this person in the dream give you?

Even a person whom you didn't see clearly may give you a bodily sensed quality.

With familiar people: Did the person look as usual?

Questions #4, #5, and #6 can be remembered together as Place, Story, and Characters.

Next, here are three ways to work further with the characters:

7. WHAT PART OF YOU IS THAT?

According to some theories, the other people in your dreams are parts of you. We aren't sure that's true, but try it out:

What feel-quality does this person give you? What sense comes in your body? You needn't name it, just have it.

If no quality comes, ask yourself: What is one adjective I could use for that person?

Now think of that adjective or feel-quality as a part of you.

If *that* is a part of you, what part would that be?

You may or may not like this part of you, or know much about it. But let it be here for the moment, anyway.

Does the dream make sense, if you take it as a story about how you relate to that part of you?

Example: Birthday Present Dream

The others in the club asked me to let Bill sleep with my wife. It was supposed to be a birthday present for Bill. I didn't like the idea, and I said she wouldn't do it anyway. In that case, they said Bill could sleep with Aunt Beth.

Associations: "That dream is really crazy. I wouldn't let them ask me something like that. I don't know what club this is. O.K., what's Bill like? Bill always does only the part of the job he likes. He is unscrupulous and imposes on everybody. Hmm...that part of me? Well, yes (laugh). But I don't like that. I'm glad I'm not like Bill. But, umm, sure, there is that part of me. Get what I want. I'd run over everybody. I don't let it come up much, even inside."

Now he fills that into the dream. "She should sleep with that part of me? Hmm."

8. BE THAT PERSON?

Stand up or sit forward on the edge of the chair. *Loosen your body.* Now imagine that you are preparing to act in a play. The play is tomorrow. Now you are just getting ready, feeling yourself into the role. You are going to play that character from the dream. *Let the feel-quality of being that person come in your body.*

You can actually do this now, or just imagine it, *but be sure to do it in your body.*

How would you walk on stage? With a stomp, or stiffly, or how? How would you stand or sit? How would your shoulders be? Don't decide. Let your body do it of its own accord.

Exaggerate it. Let's say it's a ham play. Overdo it so that the audience would laugh.

What comes to you to say or to do? Don't make it up. Wait and see what words or moves come from the body-feel.

See if you can take that with you. If you think of that character's image again, does the quality come again in your body?

These questions can be applied to any thing in a dream, not only to people. As in Charades, one can say, "Be that wall" or any object from the dream. Wait and sense what comes in your body.

(For example, you are playing the wall. You stand. Suddenly it comes to you to stretch out your arm with a stiff blocking motion, and you say, "Halt!")

You can also act your own usual way of being, as you were in the dream. Exaggerate it, see what it is when you let it be even more so.

9. CAN THE DREAM CONTINUE?

Vividly visualize the end, or any one important scene of the dream. Feel it again. When it comes back as fully as possible, just watch it and wait for something further to happen.

Wait for it, don't invent anything.

Later: What impluse do you have, if any, to do something back at the image once it has done something of its own accord?

These three questions are from Jung and Perls. I have made the role of the body specific.

One of the three is often enough. You would not usually need all three at once. You can use the other two later, if you need them.

Questions #7, #8, and #9, can be remembered as three ways to work further with the characters.

The next three questions are about decoding:

10. SYMBOLS?

What is that kind of thing anyway?

Some people think there are common symbols. Others don't agree. Try this out, and see if it opens something in this dream.

What does some object in your dream "stand for"?

Take one of the main things in your dream, and ask: What is such a thing?

What is it used for? Say the obvious.

Examples:
A bridge: it crosses from one side to the other
A river: it is a natural barrier
A policeman: an enforcer of the law
A letter: it brings a message
A tractor: it is used to plow the earth

A car: it goes somewhere

A train: it transports and can take take you somewhere, but you don't control its moving

Baggage: your clothes as well as what you take with you

Then substitute that into the story of the dream.

Dream of the Lost Baggage:

I got on a train and when it was already going fast, I realized I didn't have my baggage. I had left it on the platform.

Substitute in: You are just beginning to move or change in some way so that you don't control the vehicle once it starts. Now you realize you are leaving your usual stuff behind. Does that fit anything going on in your life?

What would you say is losing one's baggage? For example, you answer: "Then one's clothes are gone and one cannot look right. I need my clothes to make a proper appearance."

Now substitute that into the dream: You are moving in some way and you have lost your usual proper appearance? Does that fit anything?

Anything "symbolizes" or "stands for" the use, function, or usual meaning of that thing. Substitute that into the dream. See if the dream makes sense when seen or thought of in that way.

11. BODY ANALOGY? ESPECIALLY: HIGH, LOW, AND UNDER

Something in a dream may be an analogy for the body. For example, a long object may be a penis, a purse may stand for a vagina. The car may be your sexual activity. A house may be your body.

Does this fit? The attic or other high place can mean thought, being in your head, far from feelings.

Downstairs, ground level, can mean feelings, being in your body lower down, grounded.

The basement, underground, or underwater can mean the unconscious, or what is not visible.

Odd-looking machines and diagrams often make sense if viewed as body analogies.

12. COUNTERFACTUAL?

What in the dream is specifically different from the actual situation?

Exactly what has the dream changed?

Example: Wall Dream

A wall (which isn't really there) ran the whole length of my apartment, dividing it in two long halves.

If the dream went out of its way to change the situation in just certain respects, ask: Why would it make just these changes?

Or: Does the dream picture something different in value, opposite from how you evaluate it in waking life? Does someone you think of as stupid appear unusually large and impressive in the dream? Is someone pictured small, silly, or disheveled whom you in fact admire? Is something you consider worthless represented as hauntingly beautiful? See if the dream "corrects" your waking attitude. If so, try out a more moderate attitude in between.

Example: Large Father Dream

In the dream, my father came to visit, but he was huge. Linda and I just came up to his boots. And our house was tiny.

Question: "Could it mean something, if I tried out saying that he is much more important to me than I tell myself? Let me be quiet and see if anything comes to me."

Questions #10, #11, #12, are three decodings: Symbols, Body Analogy, and Counterfactual.

The next four are developmental aspects of a human being.

13. CHILDHOOD?

What childhood memory might come in relation to the dream?
If you think of your childhood, what comes?
In your childhood, what had this feel-quality from the dream?
What went on in your life at that time? What was it like for you?

14. PERSONAL GROWTH?

How are you developing, or trying to develop?

What do you struggle with or wish you could be or do?

In what way are you a one-sided, not a well-rounded, person? Could the dream or the characters in it represent what you still need to develop?

Suppose the dream were a story about that? What might it mean?

15. SEXUALITY?

Try the dream out as a story about whatever you are currently doing or feeling about sexuality.

Or: If it were a story about your ways of being sexual, what would it be saying?

16. SPIRITUALITY

What creative or spiritual potential of yours might the dream be about?

Are there dimensions of being human in the dream that you don't take much account of in your life?

Thief in a Mansion Dream

This huge mansion was full of gold and antiques. I was a thief. I went in and stole the sheets from under the bedspreads. The bedspreads were gold. I left them slightly rumpled.

What would you say is the difference between sheets and bedspreads?

"Well, you need sheets, but bedspreads are just for decoration."

Do you mostly spend your life on what's needed, with little time for beauty?

"It's true I don't have much time for things like beauty, for myself."

What about spiritual things?

"Do you mean my faith? I gave that up when I was 22."

Well, what might come if you try saying: I've mostly used everything for work and needs. Does something in me want my life to be more than that?"

Don't try to use all these questions on one dream. There are too many. Nor need you do everything you can with one question. The list is a storehouse of possible moves to make with a dream. When nothing works, the list enables you to keep going. Each question lets you generate many specific ones. They can be applied to any part of a dream. You can work with any scene, person, or thing in the dream.

Different phrasings have different effects. When a question doesn't bring up anything, saying it differently can help. You can generate various versions of each question.

Of course, you can also ask other questions that may occur to you.

Normally you will get the breakthrough and take a further step, long before you use the whole list. Therefore, don't ask them in the order they're given here; just scan the list and ask any question you like.

Appendix B will say more about each question.

For Quick Reference:

1. What Comes to You?
2. Feeling?
3. Yesterday?

    ASSOCIATIONS, THREE WAYS

4. Place?
5. Story?
6. Characters?

    THREE ELEMENTS OF ANY DRAMA

7. What Part of You?
8. How Would You Be That Person?
9. Can the Dream Continue?

    WORK WITH CHARACTERS, THREE WAYS

10. Symbols?
11. Body Analogy?
12. Counterfactual?

    THREE DECODING WAYS

13. Childhood?
14. Personal Growth?
15. Sexuality?
16. Spirituality?

    FOUR DIMENSIONS OF DEVELOPMENT

Chapter 3

The "How-To" Pointers

1. GET THE DREAM IN FULL DETAIL

Get the dream back *in visual detail*. Many people are not used to recalling or telling what they actually saw.

If it is your own dream, write it down as soon as you can. Jot down all the main parts. Then go back and write the detail of each part. What did you see? What did you feel and think?

If it is another's dream, ask the person to tell it *in detail*. You need to be able *to picture* the person's dream. It isn't really telling a dream to say, "My mother came to visit. That's all." You would ask, "Did you *see* her? Where was this? Was she standing or sitting? What did you *see* exactly?" And when that is told, ask: "Were there any other scenes? Was it just that one image?"

If it is another person's dream, say it back, bit by bit. That is the only way to retain it, and to get the time to picture it. "So, wait. Let me say this part back, see if I've got it. Your mother came to your room. First you heard her coming up the stairs, then she was inside, and you didn't see her come in. She looked upset. She was standing with the door behind her. Then she sat on your bed, and you were in the bed. Please go on."

One can work even with the tiniest scrap of a dream. A single image can lead to the whole process described here. But it is much nicer to have more.

The details are most easily forgotten, and then you have less to work with.

2. EACH QUESTION REQUIRES A LITTLE TIME

A fast answer means the question hasn't been put in touch with the felt sense yet. That takes from ten seconds to a minute.

Ponder how the question should best be put so that it applies to your dream. There might be several ways to try, one after the other. Each version can have its minute. When the dream belongs to another person, rephrase a question in various ways until you get a version the dreamer grasps and tries.

The felt sense is often slight, an ephemeral quality. You have to let your attention down into your body; you have to sense it. If you stay mobilized—"up and forward"—you cannot attend to it. Then your answer to every question will be, "No. Nothing comes."

Lie back a little. Stretch, get comfortable, take your eyes off whatever you are looking at. Let your glance go to a wall, or close your eyes (but you don't need to keep them closed). *Relax.*

If you get *too* relaxed, come back. You need to be fully active to ask your felt-sense questions and to fit what comes into the dream. Focusing is relaxed but not so deeply that deliberate doing becomes hard.

While people sense inwardly, their eyes glaze over. So, if you are interpreting someone else's dream, and the person looks right into your eyes, you might say: "Ignore me for a minute. Go inside you, and sense, *in your body,* how this part of the dream felt. Give me a sign when you get the sense of it again."

Then—when the felt sense is there—ask the question. That way the question can go to the felt sense.

At first you need to explain: *"I'm not asking you for an answer. The question is for you to ask inside, in a certain way. Put your attention down into your body and get that fuzzy sense. When you get it, please ask that question silently inside and wait. See what comes."*

The answers we want come *from* the felt sense. Or, a distinct response in the felt sense comes along with them.

Answers from your mind can be *tried out* on the felt sense. "Does that make anything stir?" "Does anything happen if I suppose...." If nothing happens, then it didn't work yet, even if the idea seems in some way right.

Try not to make up answers; rather wait.

It takes something like 60 seconds. Look at your watch sometime just to see how long that feels when we wait. But it is really so little time! So rarely do we ask the inner person, and then, when at last we ask, we don't give it even 60 seconds! If there is not an instant answer, we go away again.

But once you have waited a while, don't get locked into a tense insistence that each question must pay off. Only a few of them need to work. Give it a minute or two. Then, if nothing comes, go on to another question.

3. RECONTACT THE FELT SENSE AFTER EACH INTERRUPTION

After anything is said, you have to insure all over again that the person returns to the felt sense.

Return to the felt sense each time your mind wanders. Also, with each new question make sure there is a felt sense there, to ask. Let the question reach that felt sense.

You will notice that your mind often wanders. That's fine. Everyone's does. But every interruption also breaks the contact with the felt sense. It was here moments ago, but now it is not! Do return to the felt sense each time.

4. GET BEYOND YOUR "CRITIC"

The "critic" is that familiar part of you which frequently insults you. Freud called it "the superego." "You do everything wrong," it tells you. Or, "you're probably crazy." "If it's your own idea, it must be wrong." "You're too stupid to learn this method." Naturally it takes the same negative attitude toward your dream. It says: "This dream means you ought to stop being so lazy." (Or some other insulting and discouraging view.)

You can recognize your superego because there is an interruptive and hostile quality in it. Rather than coming out of your own feelings and expressing you, it feels like a person outside and above you, waving a finger *at* you, lecturing you, attacking you.

The effect is constriction, tightness in the stomach.

The critic is repetitious. It always says the same things, whatever may be happening. But dreams bring something new to your awareness. Therefore the critic's interpretation is hardly ever right.

All creative work, all good thinking, all dream interpretation and focusing require that the superego be put to one side. Perhaps it can be sent out to wait in the hall. If it won't go, you have to put up with it, but please: *Don't fall for what it says.* Just wave your hand at it, as if to say, "That's not news." Or, "Don't interrupt me. Let me work."

Freud asked his patients not to reject what comes inwardly, no matter how irrational or undesirable it seemed. He was quite right about this. You do need to permit them, inwardly, even if you don't approve of them, but you can decide not to act on such feelings. You need to hear more from such feelings. But the superego will interrupt, attack you for even having such a feeling. By the time the attack is over, you have lost what came. Instead you have other feelings—guilt, shame, or whatever feelings the superego attack brought on.

Then you might settle for the superego's interpretation of the dream, because you would have the feelings to go with it.

It is *very* unlikely that a dream would mean exactly the same old thing that your critic tells you all the time. If that is your interpetation of your dream, you haven't gone far enough. See what else in the actual dream is still unexplained, and work on that.

5. PRIVACY

It helps to tell a dream to someone. Often associations which you didn't get alone come even as you tell it. Having someone there also helps the silent, inward process. But this works best if you know that you can, but need not, tell what comes. Grant yourself your private space. Then telling the dream to anyone can be helpful.

Dream-interpretation is private, as dreams are. Tell someone only as much as you wish. When you interpret other people's dreams, let them know they need not tell you what comes. If they assume they should, they will block and very little will come. Tell them the method is private. What matters is what comes in them. They should say only what they want to say.

You might be curious. You might be more entertained if the person were to say everything. But if you ask for that, you won't get it anyway, and the dream will not be interpreted either. The person will feel tense and nothing will come.

The actual interpretation happens in the dreamer's private space, not in the conversation. Ask the dreamer to indicate when enough has happened, so that it's time to stop. You will hear some of it, of course, but not all of it.

If the person wants to go on working after something came, and doesn't tell you what it was, you are a little in the dark. You can't know when the dream has been sufficiently interpreted. But the person can let you know.

At first it may be confusing to work with unknown pieces, but at least you know that *something* came. If people are not free to keep silent about what it is, they won't indicate when something comes. Then they cannot take time to work inwardly with what came, since your further questions distract them. They are blocked after that, and you can ask questions endlessly. Nothing will work.

Therefore what matters most is that people feel free to tell you when something came, and to sit quietly with it until all that can come from it is fully felt. People also need time to see if the dream now makes sense. So, if the person indicates that something came, you tell them to sit quietly a while, and have it fully.

With your own dream, if you usually tell a certain person all about you, make a privacy agreement with yourself: You might tell what comes from this dream, or you might not. Later you decide what to say.

Can you feel the importance of your private space? Whatever may come is just between you and yourself. Compare that with how you would feel if you were going to tell someone instantly. Can you feel that you might not be as open inside? Less would come.

I assume that you will work mutually on dreams with someone, either immediately or after a while. Although we work alone most of the time, it helps greatly to have someone to whom to tell your dreams. You would show that person the questions, so that you could be asked them. You would divide whatever time you have in half, so that each person gets equal time. With the other person's dream you do as they direct, and with your dream you are in charge. You ask the person to behave as you find most helpful. Usually you have the person only ask you questions, and you indicate when you want them to do that, and when you want them to keep quiet.

Explain this private space before you begin:

At first, when you are helping to interpret a new person's dream, you say something like:

"What comes in you to answer these questions is private. Tell me WHEN something comes, but not necessarily what it is. Stay with each new thing silently for a while. After that you can decide what you want to say.

You can usually see when something comes. The person's face flushes, perhaps, or there is a big breath. At such a moment you can say, "Now, something came, I guess. Keep it just to yourself for a while. See how it fits into the rest of the dream. Then you can say anything you feel like saying."

In this way the interpreting process can go very deep, even if the person doesn't know you extremely well. Or, even if the two of you are very close, the interpreting can go into touchy areas. What comes will be in private space.

People may go right on telling you everything anyway, but they have heard you. Later, when something embarrassing comes, they feel free to say, "Something came, but I don't want to say what." Only when they do that can you be sure that the basic idea of privacy has been understood.

If the private space is first understood, then the more that is shared, the better.

6. ONLY THE DREAMER CAN INTERPRET THE DREAM

The interpretation comes *inside the dreamer* or not at all.

Some people think *they* can make up their minds as to what your dream means. It isn't too safe to tell your dream to people like that. They go away thinking they know a lot about you. But there are many conflicting theories about dreams. No one of them is right all the time. We use all of them to help something come. Only what comes interprets the dream. Therefore no one can decide about your dream.

Similarly, you cannot decide about someone else's dream.

Suppose you are telling your dream to some other people. Their associations are about them. These associations would mean a lot if it were their dream. Since it's your dream, *your* associations are important, not theirs. You want what comes in *your* body and resonates with thousands of *your* experiences. That's the only interpretation of *your* dream.

Conversely, your associations to another's dream don't matter much.

So don't put your notions and feelings on other people's dreams, and don't let them do that to your dream. It gets in the way.

The inward felt sense is tenuous. When someone forces foreign ideas on it, it may disappear, constrict, go back into its shell. Then that felt sense is hard to contact again, and the dream may remain uninterpreted.

When someone tells a dream in my class, I don't permit others to put their ideas on it. If they insist, I become rude and talk right at them until they stop talking. I protect the dreamer's inward felt sense.

I do the same for myself when I have told a dream. If someone begins to tell me what my dream means, I say, "Please keep those ideas a while, don't say them now." I say this loudly while the person is still talking. If I wait till the speaker pauses, my felt sense of the dream will have constricted, and I don't want that.

So make sure the dreamer knows you consider these questions

hypothetical. For example, if you say, "'Under water' might mean something hidden, that you aren't aware of...," you can add, "but it's your dream. It might not mean that in your dream."

If you have a great hunch, phrase it as a question. When you ask it, *mean* the questioning tone. You aren't only pretending to ask. You have to *ask*. You cannot possibly know. If nothing comes for the dreamer in response to your question, let it go. As with other questions, you can try several phrasings, but then drop it.

Only the dreamer's body can interpret the dream.

7. WHAT TO DO WHEN SOMETHING COMES

Something bodily opening and coming is a change process. It is you changing! But it need not be stopped after an instant. It can continue a few minutes or longer, if you let it.

Don't stop it while it is trying to change, to right itself, of its own accord, from inside. When something good has begun to come, let it keep coming.

Sometimes it expands if you just stay with it and savor it.

But it is often gone after a moment. There might have been a pulse of fresh energy, some freeing, loosening, some bit of new life—and then, seconds later, it is only a memory.

Go over how you came to this. What did you think just before which led up to its coming? As you go those steps again, ah...there it is again! Notice where the little felt shift comes. It comes *just there,* as you first think this, then picture this, and then, ah....

As you go over how it came, and get it again freshly, it may expand. More may come.

Then sense if you get to keep what came. Suppose you were to turn and think of something else, would it disappear beyond recovery, or would it stay where you could get it? An odd question, yes. But one can sense that. Some things will be gone the second you turn your back. Others give you a confidence that you have found them; they are there; you can come back to them. Concentrate on it until you get it so it will be there whenever you want to turn to it.

Spend this kind of time with anything that comes and feels good and more alive in your body. Only then go on.

8. FILLING A NEW PIECE INTO THE WHOLE

When something new has come to clarify some part of the dream, sense how the dream shapes up as a whole, now with this piece filled in. Doing that may affect how the whole dream strikes you, so that more may come.

A dream is like a puzzle. Each piece helps you clarify the whole puzzle so that other pieces may suddenly become clear.

For example, suppose you have to figure out a sentence in a foreign language of which you only know some words. You can't make the sentence out. Suppose you learn what one more of the words means. You fill that word into the sentence, trying out whether it now makes sense. It may not yet, but may be close enough so that one of the other words suddenly makes sense too. Filling that in as well, the whole sentence may become clear.

For example: you dreamed there was no way to cross a river, then you saw a bridge that went to an island further down the river. Suppose you already know what that stands for in your life, and what it is you are trying to reach. But what does the dream say about that? A little later you realize that "further down" means lower in your body, more physical, grounded. You actually used the phrase the day before in that way. You said, "Debbie is so fluttery and hyped. She needs to come down." Filling that into the whole dream, it says that your bridge is "further down," but goes to an island. As you let your attention down into your body, a peaceful quality comes there. Suddenly you know what the "island" is! It's this peaceful place inside you, alone, away from all the pressure.

With that filled in as well, the whole dream now speaks clearly. The way to get there is lower down and goes first to this peaceful island. Whew—you can feel the relief when you drop the pressure you've kept up. Yes, that's right, the tense way you were going at it can't possibly work, you realize now.

Filling one new bit into the dream may clarify the rest of it.

9. HOW TO REMEMBER YOUR DREAMS

Many people say they hardly ever remember dreams. How can they begin to interpret them when they have none? In my classes this is true of about one-third of the people at the start. After a few weeks they all remember dreams.

It has long been well known that writing dreams leads to remembering more dreams.

Keep paper and pencil by your bed. Write each scrap or bit of a dream down.

But how can you begin if you have no dreams? What can you write down? If you have even a vague sense that you dreamed something, write down: "Dreamed something." Stop a minute and *focus on the felt-sense quality* left from it. Then write that down. "I think maybe sort of funny"—or whatever fits best. *Write down something.*

If you do this, you are welcoming. You are open. You are there to receive dreams, the messages that the rest of your self sends. Soon there will be more than such vague vestiges.

If there is a vague vestige, a felt sense, stay with it. Spend a minute finding the best word for that quality to write down. That way the dream has a chance of coming back, if it will. You cannot control that, but you can give it the minute in which it can happen.

After a week or two if you still remember no dreams, set your alarm clock for various times during the night. Or take a nap in a chair. Or drink a lot of water before you go to bed so that you'll wake up during the night to go to the bathroom. Or sleep with your clothes on, on top of the bed, for part of the night. *Any way of sleeping more lightly lets you recall your dreams.*

Sleeping more lightly for a while also gets around another problem. There is pressure in the morning, taking care of kids, hurrying to work, getting going. Sleeping more lightly lets you wake before that to write your dream down.

You may need a flashlight by your bed so as not to wake others.

Some people find that writing keeps them from going back to sleep in the middle of the night, or on Sunday morning when they want to sleep longer. Then it's best to write just a note on each part, to help recall it later. Don't interpret it now. That way you can go back to sleep.

If you don't want your dream-notes read, write them in a personal code of abbreviations. Then they stay private.

These methods work. After some weeks people remember more than enough dreams. Sometimes too many. When writing them down becomes a chore, stop writing for a while.

It is a fact that people dream every night, and quite a lot! About two hours' worth! No one remembers all that, but we think (we don't know) what is remembered is the most important part. At any rate, your organism decides what you will remember. Since you do dream, you can rely on it, you can remember your dreams. They are there.

10. LOVE AND ENJOY THE DREAM, INTERPRETED OR NOT

It is good to interact with a dream, whether an interpretation comes or not. We need not interpret this dream; there will be other ones! What *is* important is welcoming the dream, loving it, enjoying how imaginative it is.

Turn the dream this way and that, enjoy its creative quality. For example, "Gee..... stealing sheets from under bedspreads. Aren't dreams wonderful? Who knows what it means, but isn't it interesting? I could never have made that up."

If we give admiration and attention to this dream, the next one may be clearer. Let me use an analogy.

Suppose a friend sends you a message. You open it, carry it with you all day, puzzle over it, but can't make it out. When you tell this to your friend, you encourage another message. On the other hand, if you say, "I never opened your letter, I just forgot it," your friend is not likely to send you another one, and surely not a less guarded, more open message.

When working with another person's dream, this needs to be said: "We don't *have* to figure it out—it helps to enjoy the dream and give it our attention."

Enjoying the dream is more important than interpreting it. Therefore, don't work so hard that it stops being pleasant and exciting.

Don't set up big pressure to "get somewhere" with it. Stop as soon as interpreting is no longer enjoyable. Just love the dream and expect another.

If it is someone else's dream, *of course* you stop the instant the person wants to. *You're a guest in that person's internal space.* Do nothing there that isn't welcome. When people enjoy it, they do it again.

Be in relation to your dreams, not just this one, and make it a good, loving relationship.

Chapter 4

The Questions Applied to Dreams

Here are some examples of dream interpretation, Stage One. I will stop at the breakthrough. Later in the book I will tell you how some of these people worked further with their dreams.

You will see how the questions are used. Note that usually a number of them bring nothing. After a while one of them brings the breakthrough.

Plastic Ring Dream

I got to my seat on the airplane. Lying right on the seat was a child's ring with different color stones. Someone had just left it there. I knew it wasn't worth anything, it was plastic with glass stones. It was definitely a child's ring. It then slipped down between the seat and the wall, and I left it there.

QUESTION #1 (WHAT COMES TO YOU?): "What comes to me is the airplane I am soon going on to my new job. The job is temporary. It's just exactly what I'd like to be doing, so I am getting ready not to be disappointed when it's over. I keep having a hope that it would become permanent. Actually it's certain not to.

"Yes, it's like that ring. It looks like gold and diamonds, but it's a child's toy."

QUESTION #2 (FEELING?): "The feeling in the dream was I wanted the ring, I was like a child. I loved how it looked, all gold and shiny. But I knew it was plastic."

QUESTION #5 (STORY?): The story summarized: "Well, first I

29

saw the ring, and then it was gone. First I saw this shiny thing, then it was gone. That summary doesn't do anything. How could I get more events out of the story? Oh, I see. First the ring was there, then I didn't take it, and then it slipped down. Hmm! *After* I didn't take it, that's when it slipped down."

QUESTION #7 (WHAT PART OF YOU?): "What part of me is that? The ring? I know. Sure. It's the child part of me! And I didn't let that be, so it went away. I keep that down in myself, out of sight. Come to think of it, I said it was plastic. I didn't really know. I figured that because it was definitely a child's ring! Hmm."

(He feels and considers the possibility that his "child part" is more valuable than he usually thinks, and that he might let it out more, keep it from slipping out of sight.)

Early Death Dream

Bob Park died. I said it was very good that he died while he was still in good health, so he could avoid the years of illness and pain.

QUESTION #1 (WHAT COMES TO YOU?): "What comes? I saw Bob on the street last week. He seemed O.K. I wouldn't say a thing like that when someone dies."

QUESTION #2 (FEELING?): "I didn't feel anything much. Umm. I wasn't sad. I don't get anything much."

QUESTION #3 (YESTERDAY?): "Yesterday I went to work. I thought some about when will I ever get to do the things I'd really like to do. I'm middle-aged and I'm not doing them. But that doesn't connect with the dream."

QUESTION #6 (CHARACTERS?): "What is Bob Park like? Well, like me, very conscientious, always well organized and doing what he's supposed to do. I wonder if he's doing what he really wants to, or if he ever will."

QUESTION #7 (WHAT PART OF YOU?): "Oh, I see. ... Yes! It wouldn't be so bad if that part of me died, that's like him. If it died while I'm still in good health and before I hit those years of illness and pain!!"

Maimed Child Dream

I am in charge of a classroom of small children, five to seven maybe. One little girl, especially attractive but mischievous, is moving towards the door—maybe intending to escape? I watch her, she smiles innocently, still edging towards the door. Suddenly she flits through it and is gone. I'm after her in a flash, pursuing down corridors. But she is fleeter than I and is escaping. I call out to the world, "Stop that child!" They slow her enough to allow me to catch her. I grab her left arm only to discover that there is no hand. It's only a stump, long since healed, but a only a stump. So I grab the other hand, with my left hand, and then start slapping her, harder and harder, so hard that I can see I have left bloody marks with my finger nails.

"At first this dream made no sense at all."

On **QUESTION #1,** what comes to mind from the day before? "I read a story about innocent suffering. Also, we were on vacation, and I didn't even start the work I took with me. We did leisurely lovemaking and hiking. I was sunning myself on the beach for two straight days."

QUESTION #2 (FEELING?): "The feeling it gives me is one I had as a child: 'I've gone too far!' Escaping from the schoolroom. I know that feeling.

"So this dream must be my self-punishment. But why a girl, rather than a little boy?"

QUESTION #7 (WHAT PART OF YOU?) "It seemed to fit that puzzle, so I take it next. What part of me is this girl?

"I remember—and I feel it again now—an old violent desire not to be a sissy that I had in school. Yes, some of my attacking her connects up now. I could have killed anybody that tried to call me a girl. I can feel how violently I am down on anything that's like being a sissy.

"What I really get here isn't the female part of me, but my anger at it."

Filling that into the dream:

"So the dream is a story about how I treat that part of me? I'm pretty ugly to it, all right.

"I guess it is feminine to indulge yourself and lie around rather than doing my masculine tasks. I have trouble letting this part of me be. I can't feel that it's O.K. to play."

Getting back to the felt sense:

QUESTION #8 (BE THAT PERSON?) "It is hard to do [trying to play this little girl]!

"Aha! It feels mischievous! Even hostile. Boy, I could sure wipe everybody out if I let go with this part. I would just be smiling and innocent (like her in the dream) but my nasty cracks would get everybody just where they ought to be got!

"Now I feel 'I went too far' (because I said I'd like to get them all). This old 'I went too far' has pushed away the mischievousness.

"I just thought: 'This thing in me can come up with the funniest, nastiest cracks if I don't stop it. *I have long ago cut this off.*' Then I realized how the phrase 'cut this off' fits with the dream!"

Nina's Dream
A bunch of kids are playing and stealing my furniture, piece by piece, but one little boy is crying. I am mad at the boy. He's three years old. He gives me three dollars. I go into the bathroom and climb out the window. Then I drive far away. It's a blizzard, very cold, snow is coming down. There are six roads at an intersection, and six women are trying to find the road home for me. But I lie down in my car, freezing. Then I woke up.

It made no sense at all until I did Question #8, being that character.

"I sat and pretended I was getting ready to play the little boy who was crying. For a while I made like I was crying, and I felt sad. Then suddenly I was imagining shouting something. And I had to laugh. I was shouting '*Piss on everybody, I'm a girl!*'

"I suddenly became a little girl as I was doing it.

"I didn't know the little boy was me. After that I figured out most of it. When I was little I had to try to be a boy because girls were no good, they were not accepted. Well, I didn't get accepted that way either... And that was what was sad, why the little boy is sad. But then (and now too, as I'm writing) that sadness flips, and there is this rush: *Piss on everybody, I'm a girl!*"

Mona's Broken Vase Didn't Spill Dream
I brought my mother a beautiful, carved, glass vase jar with liquid in it. My mother put a lid on it, which did not fit, but she forced it down anyway, so that one side of the vase broke. But the liquid did not spill out. One section of that side broke off.

QUESTION #1 (WHAT COMES TO YOU?): "That's about the part of me that's broken, because my mother didn't love me. That dream pictures just how I feel. Way inside something in me is broken. I've always felt it can't ever become whole."

QUESTION #5 (STORY?): "It was beautifully carved and my mother put a lid on it and broke it. That's me, but I don't seem beautiful to me, just a swamp, a mess.

"It's hard to feel that I had something beautiful. A little bit I can feel it.

"My mother could have liked what was in me, or somebody could have liked it. Maybe it was beautiful before it broke, but not since."

QUESTION #2 (COUNTERFACTUAL?): It's about something counter to the facts, since the liquid didn't spill even though the vase was broken.

"I thought, 'Well, usually when a vase breaks, the liquid spills out. This is pretty funny here. The vase broke and even so, the liquid *didn't* spill.'

"I had to work hard to stay with it. But I could feel something stirring in me. Then I got a big feeling that said:

"'Maybe it is still there. I guess it is still there. It didn't spill, what was in me. It's not lost.'

"It made me cry."

Chapter 5

Interpreting Other People's Dreams

What I said so far applies to other people's dreams as well as your own. But there is one great difference:

With another person you can do far less than this book describes, especially at the beginning if working on dreams is new to the person.

With someone else you need to check your welcome as you go along. Try to sense quickly when the person wants to stop or go on to a different question.

At first people may not permit you to instruct them very far. You may be able to show only a little bit of how to use the questions. Later you can tell more of how to do it. But no matter how long you have worked with the person, don't interpret the dream.

Limit yourself to asking what a dream means. Tell only how to work on a dream. May I explain this difference between how and what?

Show the person *how* to work on the dream: *how* to let a felt sense come at each spot, *how* to focus on it, *how* to use the questions inside. Bit by bit, as it comes up, show *how*.

What other people's dreams mean is their property. No one else should mess with it.

You can become an expert on dreams. But no one is an expert on another person's life. I have been a psychotherapist for thirty years. I am an expert on "how" to work with oneself, certainly not on "what" to be. When you develop skill with dreams, don't let it fool you into thinking that you can know what someone's dream means. It has meaning in that person's life. Each person, by being human, leads a life. No one can be displaced from that position.

If you grasp the how/what distinction, you can be confident that you will be helpful. *Company without intrusion is helpful. You learn the rest by practice.*

Overbearing people act like experts on life. But so do those who are too shy to say "no." If asked for an opinion, they feel they must say something. Don't be afraid to say: "Only you can answer that question. It will come from inside your body."

This may sound like voluntarily giving up power and influence over people. But what you give up is only a seeming power; in fact it gets people stuck. Real power is when you enable people to find *their* process and *their* real answers. Seeming power defeats itself and makes a fool of you.

Do not mix your stuff in. If you have a great idea, turn it into a question. Help people explore *themselves* and *their* lives.

If you are not a doctor, you might think that is the reason why you would leave steps and decisions to come in the person. But if you are a doctor or a psychotherapist, this applies even more urgently, because people put up with false power longer from "authorities" than from others. Be an authority on how, not what.

In addition to our sixteen questions, you can form a series of questions out of what the dreamer says. In this way almost anything you might want to say can be turned into questions. Use a series of questions, rather than one. You guide yourself by the dreamer's answers and use the dreamer's words, step by step. It is much better than giving your own view and closing everything.

For example, someone dreams of a lid on a pot. Let us first see what happens if you tell your own view. You say that lids might be covers or defenses like "keeping a lid on something." The dreamer agrees the lids might mean that. Nothing more happens. Now you have already intruded one step into the dreamer's territory. It will be another step to push the dreamer to try your interpretation more deeply: "What in your life are you holding down or keeping a lid on?"

Instead, suppose you only ask questions. Then you would have asked the dreamer: What is a lid? What is the function of a lid? You would then get that person's own sense and phrasing. For example, suppose the dreamer makes a circular motion with one hand, and says "A lid is something you screw down." This is much more specific and pungent, and it is the dreamer's own. Now, you are not intruding if you questioningly repeat this. "What is like that for you, something you screw down?"

You can repeat anything the dreamer says several times, pensively, helping them get more of what will come with it.

If there is a big response in the dreamer, it might be a good place to stop, unless the dreamer goes on in some way.

Another example.

All-American Perfectionist Dream
Many people came and brought presents, and things that would help me. But nothing helped because this one young man kept carrying everything out of the house.

What was that young man like? What was the feel-quality of him? "He was sort of an All-American Boy, a perfectionist."

Hmm. So no matter how much comes in, this All-American perfectionist carries everything back out. Can you sense the part of you that is the All-American perfectionist?

Here the dreamer is asked a very personal question, but it is welcome because it uses only the dreamer's own phrase. Nothing else would be better.

If you are the person's therapist, you may be welcomed to do more. You might be welcome while you ask some question five times in five ways, trying to let some hunch of yours work after all. You might be welcome to share your general knowledge or say your interpretive hunches often. But in the end the basic principle is the same. The dream and the life are that person's. A therapist who tries to force what does not—just then—make an opening can only get people stuck, blocked, and blaming themselves.

We lay the groundwork for our attitude by telling people they can keep to themselves what comes. Once they can say, "Something came...I'd rather not say what," they are safely in charge. But people need to see that it is really all right with you if they don't tell you everything. Then they are free. Otherwise they think it is impolite not to say what just hit them, and they don't let it show when something does.

Do you lose anything by letting people keep things to themselves? I have already answered that. Once they know they are in control they can let more come, and then they tell you much of it. If they block inside, neither they nor you get anything interesting.

Professional therapists have an ethics of confidentiality. They do not tell others what was told them in confidence. This professional ethics only formalizes what you will naturally feel when anyone shares private space with you. *Of course* you would not tell others what the person has shared, nor say it carelessly where others could hear it. You cannot understand dreams sensitively without prizing the inherent value of what you hear from inside people. If you don't sense that yet, obey the confidentiality rule, but expect to feel it soon.

In the How-To chapter, I also said, "And, *of course,* when the other person wants to stop, we stop." Can you see why I said "of course" in that sentence? It's the other person's dream and life. You are working on it only at their invitation. *Of course* you stop when they wish. Therefore you also stop with any given question when they wish. You stop doing anything that you are asked to stop.

But with polite people you need to observe their faces, so that you can notice discomfort. Then you can ask: "Is this not O.K.? Should we go on to something else?" Many people find it easier to say "yes" to that question than to tell you if you don't ask.

If you're not wanted to, you would not go on about that person's dream, just as you would not stay at their house after they asked you to leave. Inner space is more to be respected than a person's house.

But in return the person will have enjoyed telling you the dream, and will want to do so again. You will be trusted further. You will hear more than if you try to take charge of the other persons.

After some time and question, let the dreamer take over the process. Give the dreamer the list of questions, and ask: "What question do *you* want to ask next?" Stop directing the process and say "You go on, now, quietly or out loud, any way you want."

Chapter 6

Can Dreams Be Scary?

Many people don't know that everyone has scary dreams at times. They think something must be wrong with them. You may think that yourself.

Most scary dreams bring something good which is not yet in a form the person can use. I believe this is true of every scary dream, but our knowledge is too uncertain to permit the use of "every" and "always." I can say that when dreams I worked with were scary, they turned out to bring something which was good, but seemed bad because the dreamer had avoided it for so long.

Dreams are very flamboyant. For example, killing, death, fire, explosions—these should not be taken literally. They can indicate angry feelings that would not be too threatening if they were felt. Such images can indicate a good self-preservative energy. If feelings have been long suppressed, the image can come in the scary form of a murderer or a big fire. On the other hand, when felt in an aware way, it might be more like, "Leave me alone, I've had it with you," or, "Get out of my way."

One gets accustomed to dream language. Dreams are like fairy tales—you may get killed and be all right again soon afterwards. Someone's head is chopped off and a better person comes out from under the head.

Dreams are dramatic. In a movie, after an involved plot, let's say Mary is at last breaking up with John. Her long accumulated angry feelings come out, and it's finally over. Which would be a better dramatic backdrop for the night when this happens: a little rain or a huge explosion at the oil refinery, with fire burning the whole town?

Dreams regularly choose very dramatic ways of expressing feelings. That doesn't mean those feelings will in fact burn everything up if they come out. Similarly, the movie isn't cruel to the people of the town. The explosion happens the same night because the movie needs the *visual and sound images* so that you *see and hear* the feelings of the situation.

It takes a little while to learn the metaphorical language of dreams, but not very long. At first strange, it will soon become familiar, especially in your own dreams. In the dream you may have been scared, but in working on it you needn't be.

All right—suppose we're not scared of scary dreams—they mean something good that will expand us. It won't be in the form it first comes. Suppose we aren't afraid of wild imagery, dramatic visual expressions.

Am I saying dreams need not be feared? I think that's right. But don't dreams foretell the future? No, not necessarily. I think a dream might warn me that, *as things now stand,* a certain thing might happen. It presents a future *from here,* and gives me a chance to change something.

Dan dreamed he had an accident on his motorcycle. Does it mean he should stay off it? Probably it has greater meaning in his life—more than just the motorcycle. Probably it means that some way of living, some manner of being, might run into trouble and needs to be changed. Of course, only Dan can find out, via his body. But about the motorcycle too, the worst it could mean is, "This might happen *if* you go on doing as you have, without changing something." What did he do just before, in the dream? The dream might hint what needs to change. A dream like that is a helpful message. You wouldn't want to stop with being scared. You would want to go on to sense what it is about.

Are all dreams friendly, then? I think they all are.

Are we then never to take a dream as bad news, as bringing a limit, an end, a message we wouldn't want?

Just as I am only a part of the whole, so is the dream only a part. Neither my usual me, nor the dream *alone,* is the whole. *Neither can be trusted alone, as is.*

Therefore interpret the dream by letting it lead to a growth step. That means taking up its offer. If we take it as fixed fact, we miss that. It isn't the present facts we want, but the next growth step. This dream is exactly what "the other side" sent last night—how can it be anything but positive *if I interact with it and allow myself to become more whole?*

Truth is not static! What anything is includes what it can be, and will be. You can't explain what an egg is without mentioning what it can become. Human events and dreams are like that too. What they truly are is not a fixed thing in one moment of time. What the dream truly means may be seen only if a step occurs from it.

The negative interpretation of a "bad" dream has to be wrong because then there is no step for you as a result of the dream. Suppose you have an unfinished jigsaw puzzle and you find a piece on the floor. How can that not be positive? *But you wouldn't try to live by the bit of picture that appears just on that piece alone.* Nor would you keep the piece separately in your pocket. You would put it into the puzzle and look at *that* whole picture. But the analogy misses something, in one respect. As you fit a dreampiece into the whole of you, via your body, *the whole thing changes into something new.*

II

Something New from the Dream

Chapter 7

Introducing Stage Two: Something New from the Dream

If you practice what we have taken up so far, you will be able to know with bodily sureness what most of your dreams are about!

You will often be able to help other people know what their dreams are about.

Just that much is very exciting to be able to do. I call it "Stage 1."

Most people are puzzled by their dreams. They think their dreams are "crazy." They miss the metaphorical language. They can sense an importance, but they cannot figure the dream out.

Some people know about dreams, but only from some one viewpoint—Freudian, Jungian, or some other. They can think interpretations but cannot be sure of them. They lack the other viewpoints on dreams, and the touchstone. They settle for an interpretation that gives them a cognitive "aha," a plausible "fit," a mental hypothesis. But you can now know what your dream is about, and take others through the questions, showing them the inner touchstone. When the felt sense of the dream opens in their bodies, they won't need anyone to convince them.

But knowing what a dream is *about* is not yet a full interpretation. We can go much further.

Stage 2 is getting something new from a dream.

Something very new often arises simultaneously with realizing what the dream is about. There is an unmistakable felt shift and a big opening, which gives a step of personal change. Then Stages 1 and 2 have happened together.

But sometimes a felt shift tells what a dream is *about* (or one may know this from the start), and yet there is nothing new. It *seems* interpreted, but it says what one knew or felt before.

People say of such a dream, "It's a perfect metaphor for that situation, all right. Sure, that's what it means." And it does—*but it has not yet brought anything new*. One might as well not have dreamed it.

For example, say you are scared of a certain situation. Now you dream of a big bear chasing you. From the circumstances in the dream you know, suddenly, that it is about this situation. It feels like a bear chasing you, yes! That's exactly right! That *is* the same feeling. And now it makes sense why Joe is in the dream, standing there, very much at ease. Only yesterday you thought that Joe wouldn't be scared of this. And other details fit too. It's very exciting how it all fits. Yet, when you come down to it, you knew all this yesterday. You feel just as you did before.

The dream has not changed or taught you yet. It has not brought you anything you didn't have before.

Stage 2 is for getting something new. It comes in that bodily unmistakable way which is always our touchstone.

We don't know, scientifically, that every dream does indeed have a role to play and does actually bring something new. But we think so. You will often be rewarded if you don't consider a dream interpreted until a felt growth step comes.

Once you know how to process dreams you go quite naturally to Stage 2. If you know what a dream is about and it gives you nothing new, you say, "Aha. Now comes Stage 2," or you might go on without thinking of a separate stage.

HOW TO GO FURTHER

YOU IN GENERAL

Even if the dream is clearly about some situation it may not be *only* about that. Stay open for whatever else it is about. One dream can have many themes crossing in it, like avenues crossing one intersection.

Every experience really contains many, many experiences inside itself. You can see this at any moment you stop and get a felt sense of what is happening. It has many experiences implicit in it.

The situation (any situation of yours) is an instance of what you are like as a whole. It won't be just this incident with this person. You are this way also in many other situations. How you are goes back many years. The dream will be about you, how you are in this respect, not just about this situation.

USE MORE QUESTIONS

You couldn't have used all the questions just to know what the dream means. The remaining ones can lead you further. The questions can be applied to specific parts of the dream.

FIND PARTS OF THE DREAM THAT ARE STILL PUZZLING

Let us say you understand the bear and the person watching, but what about that odd blanket that seems to be walking in one part of the dream? If you haven't had a physically felt opening-up about that blanket, there is more to work with.

Usually one cannot, and need not work on every part of dream. But if you haven't yet gotten anything new, then yes. Go on.

There is usually some part of a dream that can lead further. The questions can be directed to that point, which may bring another step.

Whatever is still puzzling can serve for Stage 2.

In Appendix B, I will also tell you more about how to use each question.

But first we have to discuss a very large problem: Stage 2 is for getting to a "growth step," but who is to say what growth is? In what direction is change good, right, or fitting for me? We must discuss what a growth-direction is, how one can get one, and how to recognize it.

Only after that can Stage 2 go more deeply. You can't work for a growth step if you don't know how to recognize a growth-direction.

OUR PROGRAM FROM HERE

First we want to make clear what a growth direction is.

Right after that, in Chapter 10, we will clarify the BIAS CONTROL to avoid the typical pitfall of self-interpretation.

How To Get a Growth-Direction and Steps

Interpreting dreams is fascinating, of course. We do it for many reasons. One is to grow, to develop as humans. Whatever the other reasons, we would not want to miss the development that dreams can bring.

But how can I know the direction of my growth and development? If I decide what change to aim at, my decision springs from my feelings and attitudes, how I am now. When my friends hear my change-aim, they might say, "Yes, he would choose that. That's typical of him." *My own plan for my change will keep me basically unchanged. But no one else can decide for me, either.*

For example, what do you suppose very caring people choose as their New Year's Resolutions? Usually it is to become even more caring. Such people feel bad about the few self-assertions they do express. So they resolve to eliminate these as well. On the other hand, very pushy people resolve to become even more effective and successful. People decide how to change according to their present values.

The organism isn't a physiological machine that needs only physical things. The body is a cosmic system, rich in implications and directions beyond conception. In a life we develop only some of what we "are."

A growth-direction is sensed with your body. Dreams often (some people say always) bring something that can help you sense a growth direction and take a step in that direction.

Let me say how to sense a growth-direction.

FIRST: APPROACH YOUR INWARDNESS IN A FRIENDLY WAY

If you find some feeling, be friendly toward it even if you don't agree with it or like it. People say, how can I be friendly with something in me that causes me so much pain? Sometimes they say, "I know I should accept myself, but I just don't. I'm mad at myself."

One need not agree with a feeling inside to be friendly. For example, you are too afraid to do a certain thing you wish you could do. Let us say there is nothing to fear, yet you are scared and always avoid the situation. You are angry at yourself about it. Here is how you can be friendly with this fear and this anger.

"All right," you say. "I am angry at myself about that. Sure, that's understandable." You sympathize with your anger; you need not pretend you're not angry. You make a place for the anger, over to one side. Then you *separately* attend to your scared place in a friendly and inquiring way. Instead of being angry *at it,* you have placed the anger in a spot of its own. Now you ask the scare itself, in a friendly way, "What are you scared of, really?"

Putting the self-attacking to one side is something like this: Imagine that you are a school counselor. An angry parent and a child come to you. You hear the parent's accusations. "She's scared of going to school. There's nothing to be scared of. I've told her a million times. She's just stupid, she is just ... " You interrupt the parent, and you say: "Of course, that's very upsetting to you. Naturally. But please wait outside a little while. I'd like to hear from the child directly." You wait until you are alone with the child. Then you ask in a friendly way: "What's so scary, honey?"

You would know that the child might take a while to answer. She was just yelled at, and accused of this and that. Perhaps she has been yelled at for a long time. Also, she might not have ready words for what is scaring her. So you would wait in a friendly way.

The friendliness doesn't mean you agree with the child, that she *should* be scared. You don't agree or disagree. You haven't yet heard. *Outwardly* the child is scared of school. You think you know that's nothing to be scared of. But *inwardly* the child might be scared of many things you could not guess.

Approach your inward felt sense with the friendly and open attitude you would have toward the child in this analogy.

When the felt sense opens and answers, you might not agree with what it says at first. Similarly, the child might say, "I'm scared to leave my mother with my little brother because she'll forget about me." If the child tells you this, don't instantly argue! Don't say, "No, your mother wouldn't forget you, that's silly." Be glad the child was able to speak. Welcome the confidence. Say, "Oh, that's what it is. I'm glad you told me."

There is also a welcoming kind of understanding: One can say, "Oh, sure, yes, of course, *if that's what it seems like, sure you'd feel that way.* You wouldn't want to leave your mother if you think she'd forget you. Sure. Of course. I can understand that."

And then, after a while, when that much is really received, welcomed, taken in fully, when it has had your company, only then is it time for the next step. And the next step is again a friendly inquiry: "Can you sense... what makes you feel she'll forget you?"

The same friendly way would unwind what is in your own fear. Receive the little steps that come from it. Be glad it spoke, whatever it said. For example, say that after a minute your fear opens. You sense a little stirring inside, and you find, for instance, "Oh, some of why I'm scared is they won't like me." Don't instantly argue, "That's silly. Everybody can't like you." Receive it. Welcome its having opened. Say, "Oh, so that's it, is it?" Savor it, and sense whether that's it, exactly. If it is, you will find a bit of unmistakable relief inside. You gently check, "Is that right, exactly?" Something eases in there as if to say, "Yes. That's right. That's it."

If this signal of rightness doesn't come, just stay with the fear and keep asking in a friendly way, touching and tapping the fear. It may not open instantly. Perhaps it has been yelled at and cramped down in there for a long time. Eventually it stirs, opens, and tells you one step of what it is.

When your inwardness does speak, understand it. Say something like, "Oh, of course, if you need everyone to like you, that's hard. They might not. I see." (Or whatever is true here.) It is a sense of, "Sure. Of course. Yes, I see. Naturally. That's understandable. *If that's how it seems, then it makes sense that you would feel that way.*"

After that has been received, after you have welcomed its opening, after you have been with it for a while, then you can go on to the next step: In a friendly way you ask, "Why is it so important that they like you?" (Or the right next question might be different. You will sense that. For instance, it might be "Why won't they like you?")

All this is explained in more detail in my book *Focusing* (1981). There I also show how to get beyond the words, the old *ideas* that come. Your mind may often interrupt. It is as if the parent who was asked to wait outside comes in all the time. You may not be able to prevent these interruptions, but you can know the difference between what comes from the felt sense itself, as compared with ideas, thoughts, hypotheses, explanations, and sometimes accusations. If you know the difference, you can wait until you can contact the felt sense again. Only from it come the steps that make felt shifts, bits of change in you.

Each inward stirring and opening is a bit of change. Even if it only seems to say what it is afraid of, the bodily felt opening is a bit of change. In a minute or tomorrow, you can go another step. The *whole* way you are changes a little bit with each body-sensed step.

The purpose is not to find out this or that about yourself. The purpose is growth, your development. You do find out a lot along the way, but that isn't the main thing. Sense the stuck places inside, and the relief, when they stir a little, and loosen. It is as if some part of you has lived in a box—for ages. It is stiff. When it gets to stir even a little bit, that's a relief. When at last it can stand up, stretch, and move, that is a big relief.

Change has small steps. At each step the picture changes. Whatever you find out at this step will change in the next few steps. Therefore receive *whatever* you find. Don't argue or edit it. If you let it be and breathe a few minutes, the next step will let it change further.

For example, suppose you find a feeling like "It's hopeless. I can feel that I'll never be all right." Doesn't that have to be discouraging? Not if you know in advance that it will change if you receive it. Instead of getting discouraged, receive it compassionately. "Oh, sure, yes, of course that can't feel good in there, if it is convinced it can't get all right." Then, a minute later, ask it in a friendly way, "What makes it seem so hopeless?" You will soon find another bit of felt shift, with another bit of finding out. For example, what next comes is: "I have to keep trying to please her, but I know she's never pleased." Now you see that your conviction wasn't that you *can* never be all right (as it had seemed). Rather, it's that she is never going to be pleased. But that is already much less discouraging. With her, of course, that was always true, she cannot be pleased. You may need some more body-felt steps. You may still feel a longing to please her (even though you left her years ago). But you know that this will also change, in the next steps.

When we experience such change-steps a few times, we know to expect them even when we cannot imagine how a feeling could ever be different. It is a lot easier to receive a feeling in a friendly way when you know that what comes in such steps changes in the further steps.

Such steps come from a "felt sense"—how can you get and recognize a felt sense?

GETTING A FELT SENSE

A felt sense is not just an emotion. Fear, anger, joy, sadness—these are emotions. A felt sense is different, it is global and fuzzy. It includes more than the emotion—many things, most of them not clearly known.

It is a *bodily* quality, like heavy, sticky, jumpy, fluttery, tight. At first it has no fitting label. It is the way the middle of your body feels.

To let it come, first sense the middle of the body from inside. Then think of the problem, or some part of the dream. Does it feel just fine in the middle of your body? *There!* A certain quality comes in unmistakably. No. Not fine.

A dream typically leaves a felt sense. If it is already there, give it your attention. It isn't plain fear, joy, or sadness; it feels a unique way for which there is no word.

Let me show the difference between an emotion and a felt sense. Anger is an emotion. When you are angry, you recognize that. No puzzle, nothing vague, you're mad. But if you relax a little, you can sense: "There is more involved in the whole thing." For example, you may sense a breathless, hurried quality, a sense that you'd like to stay mad—you don't want to stop and see that you're a little wrong. *That* uneasy quality has no name of its own. Where would you find that? Under the anger, in it, around it, at the edge of the anger. But words like "edge" do not describe it literally. The fuzzy felt sense is in the center of your body. And it includes more than wanting to stay mad. It is a fuzzy whole, a quality.

Or, take the fear in my example above. The fear is the emotion. It is familiar. Nothing new will happen if you only feel your fear again. The felt sense is different and less intense. You can let it come by relaxing, leaning back, and sensing *in your body, the whole of your discomfort with this part of your life*. Don't think one specific aspect, rather think phrases like, "whatever goes with that situation," "that whole thing," "all about that." Referring to "the whole business" lets you sense the global discomfort in your body. Fear will be *part of it* (in our example), but not all of it. The fear has "more to it." You can sense the rest of the iceberg under the fear. You physically sense something right there, with a life of its own, not fully known to you. That is the felt sense.

You can sense that it has a life of its own if you try to talk yourself out of it. It will resist. If you say something about it, and then attend back to the felt sense, you can sense that what you said is wrong. Yet you don't know what would be right to say. You cannot control when it opens. Something comes directly from it when it opens. Or, perhaps you accidentally thought something right, and it opens in response.

A felt sense is unmistakably meaningful, and yet we don't know what it is. In contrast, we know the emotions when we have them.

A strong emotion may lead us one way, but the felt sense of the whole situation might lead us quite another way. In anger we lose track, we act from less than we know. In contrast, the felt sense brings more than we know. The difference between emotions and a felt sense is therefore very important.

In our earlier example, the fear makes you avoid the situation. Your felt sense will include the fear but may let you sense how your life would move forward in an expansive way if you went toward the situation.

If you can be inwardly friendly, and if you can also get a felt sense, then I can tell you how to distinguish a growth-direction. Here is one of its characteristics:

THE GUIDING SENSE FOR STEPS: PRO-LIFE ENERGY MOVES FORWARD

A step from a felt sense gives an inner stirring—something is glad to move and speak. That is how life-energy feels when it moves "forward." That is how the "pro-life," or forward-moving, direction feels, whatever its content may seem to be. You expand, you are more, the energy flows from inside you outward.

You can sense how this differs from doing violence to your life energy. Then it constricts. You get tight, smaller. You breathe less; you get cramped; you wilt.

This difference does not yet tell you what is right for you, but don't miss it. When you constrict, ask why, right now, there is this constricting. For example, suppose you constrict whenever you think of doing this thing you fear. That doesn't mean it's wrong and you should give up on it. But if you constrict, you would immediately ask, "Just what, about this situation, makes my body do *that?*" ("That" is the constricting in the middle of your body.) You would wait and let that unease in your body do the answering.

Suppose again it says, "Oh... yeah... If I do this, they won't like me." You might get mad and wish for a different answer. But if this one is from the body, it comes with a little relief, a bit of life-energy flows. If you get mad you will miss that little bodily signal.

A bit of life energy moves perceptibly as "it" says this.

This energy flow doesn't mean that being liked by people is a right aim. It only indicates that you are on the right road here, and what came is a step on the way. This energy flow is a guiding sense!

If you can let a felt sense come, the sense of *what is unclear,* you will find the guiding sense there.

You can feel what step is expansive and forward-moving, life enhancing, as against what feels constricting, against life, imposed on you, and closing you. Step by step you can move with this guiding sense. It keeps you on the right road.

When it backs up, you ask what just stopped it.

When it moves forward, be sure to ask and keep what just released it.

COMFORT VS. FRESH AIR

A growth step is not always easy or comfortable. It can also hurt you or make you feel anxious. But it always also feels good in a very specific way I have to describe. How can it feel painful, anxious, and yet also good?

The forward energy flow I have described feels good. But we need to sense the difference between its kind of "feels good" and mere comfort. Comfort feels good too, like turning over in a warm bed. For example, staying in a stuffy room is *more comfortable,* but going out for a walk into the cold can feel forward-moving, like fresh air! *The direction of growth often feels like fresh air.*

You can soon sense the great difference between these two kinds of feeling good. Growth feels expansive, forward-moving body energy. Comfort feels stuffy, boring after a while, limiting. Perhaps it is easier but it also has a sense of loss, giving up, giving in.

Personal growth has to do with letting your inward essence live more, expand, become freer.

Can you sense this difference? Let me ask you, where is your life blocked? Take a moment now to sense where. Do it now.

....

It doesn't take long to sense your blocked places. Usually you know them, but it is hard to do anything about them. Even a few moments of just sensing how locked they feel may be hard. That doesn't feel very good. I need it for the next part.

"WHAT WOULD COME IN MY BODY, IF...?"

Suppose you want to find out, before you undertake the effort to change, whether a certain direction really would be growth for you. Then you want to test out how something would feel, which is not yet the case. You can feel, in a bodily way, how something *would* feel:

Choose one of the blocks or life-limitations you just recalled (or think of one, now). Let us not care, right now, if every way you can think of would be wrong, immature, selfish, evil, impractical, or otherwise bad. The actual shape of it will change later on anyway. Suppose, magically, somehow, that you knew for sure that *you* could grow in this respect. I know you cannot be sure of this. Let's find out what it *would* feel like, if you could be.

Let your body feel this question, What would it be like, if you could do or be that? *What will come in your body? Wait, and see what comes.* Ask it now.

....

In your head you may quickly answer, "Yes, of course, I've always wanted this." You may say, in your head, "Yes, I would feel freer, stronger, larger...." Fine, but that changes nothing. If that is all that happened, ask the question all over again, directed at your body, "What would come, in my body, if I could ...?" Wait. ..... It takes a little while for the change to come there, of its own accord. When it comes, pay attention to the body-quality it has.

....

For example, "........Hmmm, yes! (big inhale, shoulders move back, head goes up)...It would feel...well....yes, it would be ..... hmmm, like that."

Or it might be: "Whew ....." (long, long exhale, shoulders slump, relax, easing). "Whew!"

Or did you get merely a familiar sense, more of some good way you have long known and been? Then you don't have a growth-direction here.

No one can tell you, and you cannot tell your body. You have to wait until the energy moves and it gives you the quality. Like a dream, each such prospect is unique. "Suppose I knew I could.... Yes, *that's* what would come in my body.

My phrases "sense of expansion," "energy moving foward" do not give the unique quality.

The body-energy quality lets you know a lot. You see that your body is able to be and live like that! You may have no idea how you could arrange life to make it possible, but that body-sense can slowly guide you to it.

Usually we don't allow our bodies to be in a right way unless we can *first* live that way. Most people don't even know that the body, from itself, can become more as it needs to be, before you arrange life better.

At first there are no words or actions for this *direction*. More is implicit than you can think.

Even so it is *only a direction,* not yet what you go out and try to do. For example, suppose you are a very peaceable person and you have put up with too much from someone. Now what feels bodily freeing comes with an image of smashing that person on the head. This is probably not right to do, but don't now argue with it. At another time you can review the other person's side and defend their humanity. Right now, let the energy flow in your body. You won't actually smash them on the head. Right now there is no other image that lets the body righten itself. Afterwards you can work on finding a right action.

With a new right body-energy the first action you can think of is usually impossible or wrong. It is probably in a form you wouldn't want to put into action. As in a dream it may be in a negative form. Or it may be utterly unrealistic. Do not discard it on that account! Let the body live the energy, and take your time about finding something possible that will have the energy quality of this direction.

Even the word *direction* does not work here in its ordinary way. At your next step, what seemed to be the direction may change. For example, suppose you found a new expansive way of being with the prospect of leaving your major relationship. Feel that; let it be and breathe for a little while to enable a next step. For example, at that next step you may find that, no, you need to risk being different in this relationship. In the ordinary meaning of the word "direction" that would not be the same direction. At the first step you were leaving; at the second step you are staying. But for that body quality it would be another step in *that same* "direction."

The life-energy flow only indicates that this little step is on a right road. The form may change many times before there is a practical result.

Therefore the first seeming content must not put you off. It will change in form. Let the bodily energy-quality tell you its right direction.

So far I have told how to recognize a growth-direction.

Now let me give examples of finding a growth direction *in a dream.*

Chapter 9

Introducing the Bias Control:
How To Get a Growth-Direction from the Part of the Dream You Don't Like

Let me first give some examples where you would not need the BIAS CONTROL. Sensing the growth-direction is easy when a dream indicates it with beautiful living symbols:

She decided to leave her husband, almost for sure, last night. Then she dreamed a dream about daffodils:

Daffodil Dream
Someone gave me a bouquet of daffodils, beautiful ones that really glowed. And then I saw my husband also wearing one in his lapel.

She said: "At least for the moment something odd in me is moved in response to him, and I shouldn't turn away from that."
Another example comes in the tiger dream:

Tiger Dream
I was walking down the street with my father, and a tiger was walking next to me on my right, on the street side. The tiger was tough and full of energy, very beautiful. Then he turned at a right angle, crossed the street and disappeared in an old apartment house, and I continued on with my father. The sidewalk got narrow, very tiny. A big truck came and there was no place to go. It hit me or almost hit me, I don't know which.

Here the growth-direction is clearly the tiger. With Questions #7 and #8 he made inward touch with the tiger, but only a little. The plot of the dream (Question #5) enabled him to sense clearly: "That strong alive toughness goes a different way, and I keep going the way I've been, *with my father.* The old familiar drag. When I stay in relation to my father, that aggressive force stops walking with me. Soon it comes *at* me instead, and runs me over."

He could sense a growth-direction: to leave off walking with his father and be the tiger instead. That was not just an idea. He could sense the tiger-image in his body, very immediately: The excitement of the tiger was clearly different in his body, compared with "the old familiar drag."

Great beauty, or obviously healthy, energetic animals easily give us the life-instinct direction. Of course the form of living it is up to us to develop over a period of time. We won't act like tigers in every way. In these examples *the direction* is clearly given—especially if we don't put it into words.

EXAMPLES OF A GROWTH-DIRECTION FROM THE "BAD" PART OF THE DREAM

THE TIGER DREAM

With the tiger dream, above, perhaps you didn't immediately agree with me that a tiger is such a beautiful thing! Certainly some people might think, "A tiger? It might eat me." But in this example the tiger seemed beautiful to the dreamer, and also walked along with him very peaceably. In many dreams much the same tiger is ugly and menacing. Would you recognize it as a good thing?

The growth-direction is often in something that seems bad. Of course, it is a *new* development. Since we have already developed in the directions we think of as good, what we have not developed is lumped in with the bad. So it comes at first in a negative shape. It may look bad.

The Israeli-Arab Dream

An Israeli was saying, "The Arabs are two miles from our border and that is completely intolerable." In the dream I felt that the Israelis always see only their own side, only what is intolerable to them. They never see the other's side.

Associations: "Well, I'm a Jew, but I don't like the attitude of Israel. They do mostly see only their own side of the picture. They are *so* self-righteous."

Do you usually see the other person's side?

"Yes, I usually see that first. I often forget my own side. [Laughs] It's often funny, I can forget that I want something too."

Well... how would it feel in your body if you were a little bit more like that Israeli who thinks only of himself? Sense that in your body, is it a right direction?

"I hate it. I've criticized it for years. I'm glad I'm not that way. I don't want to be that way."

Well, this isn't about Israel; try it out as being about your own way of forgetting yourself. Would something stir in your body if you sensed being like that a little?

"Hm. Well.....[focuses] yes! That's right, oh, I see!"

Stay with that in your body, for a minute.

"Hmm. ....."

Can you hang on to that opening?

"Sure, I just think of this Israeli. They have too much of that, but for me a little bit would be good."

Here life-energy moved in his body in a way that felt right. Right for him, given what he had developed in his life and what he had left undeveloped.

You will see later just exactly how the BIAS CONTROL enables you to sense a growth-direction in what is at first negative. In this example please notice that the person did not find it alone. The BIAS CONTROL will often let you do alone what was done for this dreamer by the other person who said, "This isn't about Israel; try it out as being about your way of forgetting yourself."

A growth-direction is not always the opposite of what you thought, but often it is. It isn't always in the part of the dream you reject most, but it is often in just that part. The growth-direction may have a very unattractive form in a dream. It may be objectively wrong, evil, threatening, and quite undesirable. Yet, if we ask how it might represent something needed inside you, what is needed can come in your body very quickly—*and very positively.*

Question #14 asks about what is now an edge in your development. Of course, you answer with a direction you already know of. If you have recently discovered it, your dreams can show your progress and help with a next little step in that direction. Then, of course, you would not look for the opposite.

But a *new* growth-direction is often the opposite of what we value most. This doesn't mean we change our values to the opposite, not at all. We merely expand them a little. You will see that in the following examples.

For instance, you dream of a killer chasing you. A rotten or obnoxious person or a wild animal is after you. Of course it is not your growth as a person to become a killer, a rotten person, or a wild animal. And yet, if you look in that direction, a very positive new quality may come in your body. For example, it might be an energy to go after the things you need. Or it might be a new ease. It might be some sound instinct. Of course it may not, but it is likely. Why does that come so often from the opposite of what we thought?

It is because when we consciously exclude what is bad, a lot more than that gets pushed away. We exclude violence, for instance. But a lot more than we know is excluded along with it. What gets split off is not only the bad thing that shows on top.

Not all fighting instinct is bad, for example. But exclusion works all in a lump. For example, if your organism's fighting energy is excluded, you live with too little self-assertion. Then you are likely to dream the missing energy as a killer or a dangerous animal chasing you. That does not mean your strengths are dangerous. It only means that in their present form, *cut away from you, they seem to have this negative form.*

Of course! If you had fighting energy running around *all by itself,* without your wisdom and sensitivity, it wouldn't be good.

And, also, if that separated fighting energy were not yours, if it turned around and came after you, that would scare you. If this scare were pictured, what do you suppose it would look like?

That is why a growth-direction often emerges from just the most evil or repulsive part of the dream which we rejected out of hand.

Addressing all the questions to your body, you can contact *your* new energy, which can come. Especially Question #8 (how you would act in that role) can be tried with any figure that seems negative in the dream. But even a simple association can let you do that, as we saw in the last example. His association to Israelis let him ask, in his body, how being more like that would feel.

MARK'S DREAM

Mark is trying to break into show business. He wants to act, but meanwhile he has a job delivering messages, racing all day on the Los Angeles freeways. He has gotten no chance to act and feels great pressure to make good. The day before this dream he was in a producer's office, but only as a messenger to bring an envelope, and he later dreamed:

> *I was in that producer's office again, only now there is an audition. I am standing in line with others waiting my turn. A hand comes stretched out, holding a platter. I don't remember what was on the platter. It is offered to the man standing in line before me, and he turns it down. Next it's offered to me. I turn it down too, and I say, "No, not me either."*

Mark already knew what the dream was about—his wish to break into acting, or at least to audition. He had wished he could use the delivery to ask the producer for an opening, of course. So far this dream told him nothing new.

Question #8 (Be that person?) broke through: "Be the hand holding the platter." He acted it. He found himself saying, "Here. You can have it. Relax. You're O.K. the way you are. Be a slob. Don't worry. Just be satisfied with yourself."

Now it was very clear what the hand was offering, and the shift it made in his body.

"It would sure be nice, being O.K. with myself again!" he said now.

I wanted him to stay with the shift a while longer. But very quickly he said, "No, that would be comfortable, but I reject it. I don't want to be a slob."

So in the dream he rejected what the hand offered. In interpreting it, here, he rejects it again.

Now here is where he would need the BIAS CONTROL. Stage 2 is about learning something, being different, having something brought to you, something that you don't yet have as a conscious self. Naturally, then, it will be hard to recognize! If you could recognize what you lack, you probably wouldn't lack it. When it appears in the dream, your dream-self rejects it, and when you wake up and think about it, you are likely to reject it all over again.

You need to ask your body about the bad-looking part in a dream: *How might there be something in THIS which I need?* Having asked, don't answer the question! Only your body can give you something new, neither your old way nor this thing in negative form.

When it comes in you, it will change the form it has in the dream. Then it also gives you more ways to think about it. In my example, as long as Mark can think of what is offered only as "being a slob," naturally he will reject the offer. But what actually came in his body for a moment was not being a slob, but liking himself again. Yet he thinks of liking himself under present conditions as being slob. But is that the only way to think about it?

"Well...uh... I have been under terrific pressure. I deliver messages at 70 miles an hour all day. I'm so strained I'm beginning to forget things, and I never used to. I feel like, how long will it take 'til I get what I came here for? I've been here a year and I'm a messenger. I haven't had one audition yet."

In describing how he has been, Mark shows that he does need something from what the hand offered. Look back over his statement here and see if you agree with me.

For a moment Mark had felt deeply, in his body, the hunger to be all right with himself. But there is also the hurt and anger of having failed so far, and the pressured (but right) feeling that he shouldn't give up and be a slob.

"I can't settle for failing!" he said. "That's not right."

This part of the dream had brought something. The inward felt shift had been there ("to be O.K. with myself again!"). But despite that moment's deep-felt rightness, Mark could not see his way to keeping it. It meant settling for failure to him.

So we continued:

Take your usual conscious way one step further, I said (the last part of Question #8).

"Do you mean exaggerate it?"

Yes. Overdo it. What would it be if it were much more so? "... [focuses] ..... Oh, I know. [In an odd voice]. Move, feets, yeah, move feets. Massa give you an extra potato. Move, feets. Time to change that lane, has too many cars in it, that other lane faster. Work harder. Somebody maybe give you some money ..... Ooch. It's degrading ... [silent time]."

And what would the other side be, if it went one step further?

"One step further of that would be Ron."

What does Ron stand for?

"Ron doesn't give a shit. He doesn't get tense, and yet he gets his way. I'd give anything to be like Ron! ... [focusing] ...."

Can you sense it now?

"... [Focusing] ..... And how!!"

Is it Ron?

"Yes, well no, sort of. It's me taking some room, maybe liking myself again!"

THE WHOLE CONSTELLATION MUST CHANGE

Is the offering hand right, which says he ought to take it easy and be comfortable? Or is he right that he ought not to accept failure? Of course both, and neither. The right step comes in the body, from his opposite, but when it comes, it isn't just that opposite.

What we are as conscious people is cut out from a larger whole. If you cut one piece out of a pie, the rest is a circle with a gap which has that same shape.

If a little face is cut out from a big piece of paper, that face is also left on the edge of the paper. If the face you cut out has a sharp nose, so does the inverse face of the paper. (In German, "the shadow side" is a common phrase.)

Mark is cutting. His distinction is between getting somewhere and being a slob. He is a person who will get somewhere. But by the way he defines himself, he leaves the opposite face behind him, that of the slob, the person who fails to get anywhere. That slob is the inverse of the way Mark defines himself. But this is only one and the same single cut: getting somewhere, divided from not getting somewhere. But what we are not is always vastly bigger than what we are. What Mark is, is getting somewhere. So, everything Mark is not looks like "not getting somewhere," being a slob.

The slob is the whole remainder of his being with the shape of "getting somewhere" cut out of it. *Everything* in his organism, in his body, in his essence, that doesn't fit "getting somewhere" is relegated to the slob. Liking oneself, valuing oneself, letting oneself play and breathe, being kind with oneself, sensing values higher than success, all this falls to the slob. So the slob is not just a slob! The slob is a whole wealth and richness, *everything* Mark is missing in life.

Does this mean Mark should be a slob? Of course not!

Does it mean Mark should go right on harrying himself, being angry and pressuring himself, whipping himself to try harder? Of course, not that either.

When there are two characters in a drama, like the hand and Mark (or the slob and Mark), we must not choose either. Rather, the step we want brings a change in the whole drama. Then the characters will be different ones.

The slob-and-Mark are *one* constellation, one way the whole is now cut. *If one of them is not just right, the other one cannot be just right either. They make up one picture, one pattern, one cut.* One of them cannot change without the other. Both change, or neither. If there is change and growth, both change.

Therefore it would be foolish to try to choose: Does the dream mean he is right to reject what the hand offers, or does it mean he should accept it? Neither, neither!

What counts is to sense the growth-direction. And the growth-direction will be neither of these two alternatives as they are now cut. But it is probably to be found in what is now lumped into the form of this "slob."

Can you sense the growth-direction in this example?

I ask this question because, as you will notice, I have not exactly *stated* what Mark's growth-direction is! Let me explain why not.

WHEN A GROWTH-DIRECTION IS NAMED, IT IS BEST TO SAY, "SOMETHING LIKE THAT"

You can probably sense that how Mark has been isn't just right. There is too much racing, pressure, driving, and self-condemning, *something like that*.

You can probably also sense that the growth-direction is what he said about being O.K. with himself, liking himself, living well, being at ease and more confident, *something like that*.

As long as we stay with "something like that," we can sense it quite clearly!

Whatever words we use, we get a big felt sense with them. If we say "something like that," the big felt sense can stay. If we limit the growth-direction to exactly what we say, and only to that, the big felt sense leaves. For instance, sense what goes with "being O.K. with myself"—a whole large way of being and acting. But if you take the statement narrowly, it might just mean some sort of self-approval that might not even be true.

We go wrong if we try to say exactly what the growth-direction is, intending to stick literally to a statement.

And Mark too will go wrong if he tries to state it in words. For Mark there is another reason. He can think or say this only by using the old concepts he already has. But these are part of how he is *now*.

The dreamer needs to know that a growth direction cannot be defined clearly. It is rather *whatever* would be right, what is forward, pro-life, expansive. Using words like "whatever would be right" or "something like that" leaves an opening into which the growth-direction can come.

If Mark thinks of the growth-direction in this open way, then he knows that it cannot be giving up. Giving up feels closed and hopeless, dull and dead. That's not a growth-direction. That's the part of the slob which is clear. He would not let himself be stopped by the fact that the hand offers him being a slob. Of course just being "a slob" is not it. Rather, he would ask about being a slob, how could "something like that" be what I need?

If he lets his body give him *something like* the slob, what comes is very different from accepting failure. Therefore it is important to know: *Before it comes in the body, one cannot define exactly how it will come. But one has to be willing to be that negative, at least for a little while. Therefore, be the slob and expect "something like that" to come.*

After the energy moves in his body and gives a right step, it must also be left without exact definition. It is that bodily way of being. You can see that the words are insufficient. Later in the day these words probably fail to bring the new energy back. But the dream-image can bring it back, in a bodily way.

Or, in Mark's example, thinking of Ron is probably the best way he can let the right energy come again in his body.

From that new way of being also come the more practical steps of living, which we don't have at first. First one brings back the right energy, then one can often think of action steps that go with it. At first these actions may be small, different only in manner and quality. But that soon makes larger differences.

What will Mark do about this growth-direction? He called it "being O.K. with himself again." What follows for action? Perhaps more play, higher values than success, less caution not to offend people, less pressure, more risks, more of him allowed to come out, more spontaneity—*something like that.*

The first "thing to do about it" is to carry the dream image (or Ron) with him and to take a few minutes now and then to let it come in his body again.

HAVE THE SHIFT, OVER AND OVER, BY RECALLING THE DREAM IMAGE

During the next few days, Mark often recalls the dream image that gave him a growth-direction. At red lights or when the freeway slows, Mark can recall the image of the hand, offering. He can sense Ron. He can re-contact the physical shift. His body gets a chance to change, to process, to be this.

He waits a few seconds for that new way of being to come again in his body. He has the change, the felt shift, over and over again.

He lets his body be that way (something like "being O.K. with himself") regardless of success or failure. Naturally he is more likely to succeed. He enters situations with more ease and other people sense him more vividly. Some people will like him. Perhaps everyone liked him before, but only because he tried not to disturb them.

Above all, he becomes a deeper, more developed person than the success-hound he was. He does not oppress everything human in himself in that tense way. Something like that! I am only telling one way it might go.

Of course he is quite far from this desirable condition. In fact, he is so far from that, as yet, that he is likely to think, "That's how I'd like to be, but I'm not." But the step from the dream did let *that* come now, at this time—*his body can already be it, now.*

Many people miss this fact. The dream is theirs, after all. If a dream image (like the hand in Mark's dream) makes a new bodily way of being, that is their own, too. If it comes in Mark's body, it's Mark's, isn't it? Yet he might go on saying, "I'm not like that, I wish I were like Ron." We would remind Mark that the dream was made by Mark's body, and that his body just was, and therefore can be, the new way of being. That way of being is already his own.

He can let it flow again, have it again every time he thinks of the hand-image or Ron and waits a few seconds with his attention in his body. ......Ah...there it is again.

Real change is bodily. Thinking alone does not change us, although it is a vital human power. Without thinking we don't get far either. But there is a thinking that leaves an opening for the body to speak too.

Real change takes time and many little steps. The dream image brings the felt shift again, time after time. You can see that the body is not yet done processing it.

There will be other dreams and little steps from focusing. Everything is not resolved in this one felt shift from one part of one dream. It is a step. Development consists of little steps.

Long before he absorbs this step fully, other dreams will give him other similar steps to feel and be. He will see a progression in these steps.

EXAMPLES OF GROWTH-DIRECTIONS

Since a growth-direction is a bodily sense, and not words or ideas, my statements are only suggestive. Can you imagine how "something like" each of the following might be growth-direction?

Development occurs on some human dimension which the person has not yet developed. Therefore, what is growth for one person is old hat, or may even need toning down, for another person. You will find that you have more than enough of some of these items. But, can you see how each example might be growth for some person?

For each item below, imagine a person who has developed much else, but not that. Can you sense life moving forward, when "something like that" comes in someone who has lived many years without that something?

Speaking up for yourself
Trusting the way *you* see it
Reaching out for someone
Trying to do something you haven't been able to do for a long time

Exploring
Meeting new people
Being sexual
Coming down to earth
Permitting yourself to do something really well with all the care it
    takes
Letting yourself really learn something
Trying something new
Taking charge of a situation
Telling people how you need them to be
Hoping
Refusing to give up
Grabbing what you want and enjoying it straight out
Not being sick any more
Not being helpless any more
Feeling you can be cared for
Feeling that you don't have to deserve it, in order to get something
Being a separate person, in your own right
Not taking all the blame
Letting go of parents
Being angry
Not being resigned any more
Being what is stereotypically "male" and running things
Being what is stereotypically "female" and receptive
    (both of the last two can apply to everyone)
Admitting defeat and starting over
Getting peaceful
Looking around rather than running
Letting another person in
Letting it be O.K. to feel some way
Doing or not doing something because of ethics
Feeling I have control of myself in this, for a change
Seeing straight, because I'm not angry any more
Stopping myself, saying, "Wait a minute, maybe they have a point"
Having a sense of cosmic significance or mystery
Having a peaceful time
Letting someone see you as you are
Being honest
Being able to ask for help
Letting it be O.K. that you love someone

Chapter 10

The Bias Control

The previous chapter has already explained the BIAS CONTROL; now we need only state it more formally.

Even if you have found something new from the dream, don't stop without the BIAS CONTROL. What comes with it may give you a very different and more convincing interpretation of the dream.

Your first interpretation may not be plain wrong. Let us say it is right, but only one kind of "right." You have probably put your usual attitudes on the dream. We don't assume that your attitudes are just wrong. If you learned something bodily right from the dream, keep that. But if it is pretty much in line with your attitudes, don't stop with that. Look also in the other direction.

The BIAS CONTROL has two parts: The first is only a preparation, a move in *thinking*.

THE BIAS CONTROL, PART 1: FIND THE OPPOSITE INTERPRETATION BUT DON'T ADOPT THAT EITHER

Here is how you can find an opposite:

a) *In your interpretation:* Is what you say about the dream like something you usually say? Have you heard it before? Are you expressing your usual values and feelings in saying that? If so, what would be the opposite values and feelings? Just think them, tentatively.

b) *You in the dream:* If you reacted in your usual way in the story, what would be the opposite reaction? Just think it, tentatively.

c) *The others in the dream:* Find the characters and parts of the dream that are most objectionable to you, or most different from you. What about them is most clearly other than you? Assume that you might

have too little of some way of being they have too much of—don't decide
what it might be. Leave that blank.

These ways usually point to just one opposite. Most people *interpret*
a dream in the same way they *reacted* in the dream to the *other characters*.

For example, you dreamed of someone trying to break into your
apartment. Let's say you know what that stands for in your life. You
think of it as a bad thing in your life, to be prevented. In the dream-story
you had the same reaction and you double-locked your doors. So your
reaction is the same in life and in the dream-story. Now you are likely
to interpret the dream that way also.

The opposite interpretation is that you need (something from) this
thing.

The opposite action in the dream would have been to turn toward
it in some way.

The most opposite character is whoever is after you. How might you
need to be a little more like that? But don't decide what that would be,
leave that open.

Don't adopt an opposite interpretation. Just leave it open.

In the last chapter we saw that a growth step is neither your usual
way, nor simply the opposite. Mark's pressured way is not good, but a
slob is not good either. Don't try to adopt the opposite. What you want
is this: Since the opposite sits on top of "everything else" (everything
you are not), you make room for *something, as yet unknown,* to come
in your body *from this opposite.*

Part 1 of the BIAS CONTROL *leaves you with a general sense of an
opposite direction, and you leave open what possible good could be in it.*

Before I give detail on using Part 2 of the BIAS CONTROL, let me
illustrate this first part.

Recall a dream you have interpreted. Notice that you have (probably)
interpreted it with your usual attitude. Even though you learned something new, isn't it pretty much in the direction you usually go anyway?
*Try the opposite direction, not as a way to be, of course, but only to
open yourself to something positive that might later come from this negative direction.*

Most investigators say we cannot interpret our own dreams. After
all, we impose our attitudes on anything that comes along—events, other
people, new experiences, and so, of course, also our dreams.

With great regularity people interpret their dreams to say what they
thought anyway. The examples in this chapter will bring this home. But
consider:

The dream is a drama about something in your life. The drama occurred in your body. The dream told *this* story while you were unconscious. Had you been conscious, you would have directed it otherwise. It is interesting, even fascinating. It is also very puzzling. You could not make this up deliberately, if you tried. Do you think the puzzle is solved if you make the dream say what you thought anyway?

Something or someone in the story goes counter to your usual thoughts and feelings. But what goes counter is also you: These puzzling characters, so different from you, where do they come from? They were made...from you! They are from your body and still in it, now.

Therefore the BIAS CONTROL is likely to pay off. With the BIAS CONTROL you go looking for that, in the dream, which is the opposite of your usual attitudes.

You find the opposite of your first interpretation.

You also find the opposite of how you reacted in the dream-story.

You control your tendency to reject the other characters.
You prepare youself for something positive *but as yet unknown* coming in you from the opposite direction.

What is in this dream that you usually suppress, reject, or lack in yourself? What in the dream do you despise? What do you most want to get away from? What in the dream threatens you?

Open the possibility that *something* you need could come from that side, but without deciding exactly what that would be.

Here is the typical example. Something scary is chasing the dreamer from behind. He assumes it is bad and dangerous. Then, when he knows what it stands for in his life, he agrees. Yes, that aspect of my life is to be avoided. His first interpretation in this mountain cabin dream leads him to try even harder to escape it.

Mountain Cabin Dream
I was up in the mountains with Sandy. She was in a cabin that stood all alone, further down. I was walking toward it. From behind me a man came with a knife. I knew he was dangerous. I was hoping to reach the house before he got there, but he started running. He ran past me, toward the cabin. I woke up.

"I can feel that that's my anger at Sandy. I'm scared it will get out of control I guess. I am scared it will get to Sandy and I won't be able to stop it. It will break us up. I can feel that the dream is a warning to me about blowing up at her."

This example is typical of how people interpret their own dreams. It is very natural with one's own dream. And such an interpretation fits convincingly. He is probably right that the dream is (at least partly) about that. He can sense that it is about his anger which threatens to blow. But he interprets the dream in the same way that he views the situation. He controls his anger. Resentful remarks slip by him, and he wishes he could stop those too. He thinks the dream warns him not to blow up and break the relationship. After the dream he feels no different than before.

His interpretation was, "The dream is warning me about blowing up at her."

His reaction *in* the dream is the same as his reaction *to* the dream. He runs away from the man with the knife and wants to keep him away from Sandy.

Now he applies Part 1 of the BIAS CONTROL, as he makes room for an opposite interpretation.

a) "The opposite of my interpretation? It would be that I ought to blow up at her, maybe end the relationship."

b) "The opposite of my action in the dream-story? I guess I would turn and fight him, or check him out."

c) "What character or thing is most opposite to me in the dream? Well, that guy, of course. What characteristic of his is most opposite to me? Violence. I've never wielded a knife. It's not like me. I never hit anybody.

"So the opposites in a, b, and c come to the same thing: anger, violence, I guess. I'm supposed to stay open to something I need in this. The character has too much of it. Could I try saying I need some of that in a different form?"

Now, notice: It isn't too hard to think this far, but then it's a struggle to keep that open!

He thought: "Sure, there might be some mature form of anger or aggressiveness that I could use more of. But the way *my* anger is, it's no good. The dream can't be telling me to let *that* anger loose. It's immature, resentful, and destructive. I have lots of that, I don't need more. I say things to Sandy because I feel resentful. It makes our interaction bad, and then I feel bad. And the dream warns me that it could all blow up."

Here he got right back to his first interpretation. That happened because he tried accepting the simple opposite (letting his anger loose). He forgot that the point of the BIAS CONTROL is not to adopt the opposite but to stay open in that direction.

The growth step is not violence or breaking up with Sandy. Nor will it be the simple opposite of controlling his anger.

We won't make the mistake of asking: Who is right, he, himself, in the dream, or the man with the knife? Neither is likely to be just right.

We expect a *new step from the anger side, a better way than he now knows. Something like that. For example, he might stand his ground more often, become more confident, express more bad and good feelings. Who knows? He needs to leave it blank.*

What if you *recognized* the same growth-direction you have been getting recently?

Suppose Mark has another dream in which there is another image that his body senses as something like "being all right with myself." Obviously, if he recognized that, he doesn't need Part 1 of the BIAS CONTROL. That is already an opposite of his usual pressured way. He would go directly to Part 2 and let his body-sense give him the new step from this new dream.

There is usually a long series of dreams that give *something like* the same growth-direction, each dream giving a new image to work with. You will sometimes see these immediately, sometimes not. It will surprise you how often you will still need to use BIAS CONTROL, Part 1, to recognize it.

THE BIAS CONTROL, PART 2: LET YOUR BODY-SENSE GIVE YOU THE STEP FROM THE OPPOSITE

How?
I will present many ways to use.
First I will tell the fastest.

LETTING YOUR BODY BE IN A NEW WAY

A new way to be can come directly in the body. The step *might* come quickly, as in Question #8 (being that person). You sense how your body would "be" this dream-character, but what comes is *your* new way. You set your body to play the role of that dream-character exactly. Yet what you get is yours and new. It won't be just the old opposite. That's the fastest way. Our example continues in this way, but after that I will tell you many other ways.

Mountain Cabin Dream, continued:

"O.K. I'll *be* the man with the knife. How would I play him on stage? ..... What would come in my body? Wait for it to come.

"Hmm..... That *isn't* anger, exactly, and it feels good! I'm umm..... I'm going after somebody! I'm leaning my shoulder forward and, it's like I'm saying, 'Hey, you! You're gonna listen to me.' And, whoever it is gets pinned, right there."

Here he could recognize instantly that he wants this bodily way. But sometimes a person is so condemning of the missing part that it seems negative at first. I assure you that freeing it up, letting it live in your body for a minute, will let you sense a quality you will like. It won't be just what you wanted to avoid.

See what comes when you try to sense that suppressed part of you, when you let it live for a moment?

Please notice: He played a character that is his opposite, a way of being that *he usually isn't*. He played the role of the man with the knife. The dream-image directed his body how to play the role. Notice how different that is from just letting loose his familiar, resentful anger.

If he were himself a physically violent person, he would not have defined this as his opposite.

With your own opposite, put your judgment aside for a while. You won't go out and act on this part. Body energy-feeling is totally different from action. You just want to sense it for a minute. Perhaps it will come in a good, freeing, life-enhancing way. Granted your "critic" will call it bad, but sense: Does it feel like more life in your body? Isn't something grateful that you let it come alive? If so, keep it a while. Action choices are something else. Assure your "critic" that you will later find good, rational, ethical, responsible, realistic ways of action. Sense this part again and again.

Sometimes this direct way doesn't fit, doesn't come, or you may want slower ways. At any rate there are other ways. Everyone needs these at times.

LISTENING FOR THE SLIGHT, BUT DEEP, SIGNAL

If you have only an idea of something you might want from an op-posite, you can check the idea with your body. Wait for at least a slight response your body might make.

Sometimes there is a little body release in just considering the pos-sibility: Might you some time want to begin to try out whether you could perhaps touch that in yourself—just to see if there might be something there?

If you have such a slight bodily opening-up, check in with that little opening-up often during the next few days.

Although it seems of slight intensity, it can be very deep. Assume it is like someone who fell far down into a mine shaft. Although you hear only a very slight knocking down there, certainly you won't ignore it and go away.

Such "places" open slowly, in a very deep and good way, after a while.

LISTENING TO THE RESISTANCE

Suppose the prospect of playing the role of this character or thing gives you an intense reaction of fear or dislike in your body? Suppose the very thought of doing it gives you a strong physical feeling against trying it, long before you try?

In that case welcome *this* bodily response. Be friendly and understanding with it, and see more of what it is.

You need to know that *your body's step* from the opposite would not be in the form you're touchy about it. The trouble with not immediately trying for the body-step is that you don't find out how different it is from what you fear. So you might continue to fear and avoid that opposite in its old form. Going directly lets you have the new form right away.

Nevertheless, don't bulldoze the touchy feelings—just don't run away. Stay, and sense what is touchy. Give it plenty of patience and understanding. Let what is touchy talk to you and tell you why it is touchy. Going on can wait.

Give it a long and gentle hearing over the next few minutes (or days). Every time you bring that dream-image back and think of playing that role, you can get that feeling again. Don't assume you know all of why you don't want to play it. There are always *many* little steps that come, one after the other, and change the whole thing at each step.

The next few steps for a person may come from such a touchy resistance. If you feel it in a bodily way, then *that* is your body's response here. That is our touchstone. That is what working with the dream brought! Don't ignore it by running away and dropping the dream. Listen to it. Let it tell you what it is.

JUST KNOWING NOT TO FALL
FOR THE FIRST INTERPRETATION

Sometimes the BIAS CONTROL does no more than keep you from what had seemed a sure conclusion. That alone is valuable.

Even if you cannot get a bodily response from the opposite, at least you need not wholly fall for the typical wrong conclusion.

HOW TO USE SOME OF THE QUESTIONS, ESPECIALLY FOR BIAS CONTROL, PART 2

QUESTION #5 (WHAT IS THE STORY-PLOT OF THE DREAM?) can be used this way:

Summarize the story so that *your reaction in the dream is one of the events:* Say the event just before and just after your reaction.

"First he came running, *then I ran away from him,* then he got by me.

"First the ring was there, *then I said it was worthless and I didn't take it,* then it slipped out of sight" (Plastic Ring Dream, Ch. 4).

SEE IF IT MAKES ANY SENSE TO SAY THAT BECAUSE YOU REACTED AS YOU DID, THE NEXT THING HAPPENED AS IT DID.

That gives you an "opposite" interpretation, but in a different way. Now you don't interpret the whole dream by calling the ring (and what it stands for) plastic and worthless. You see that this very reaction of yours is part of the story in the dream, and *you let the dream tell you what happens* **as a result of** *that reaction.*

Since the typical reaction to a dream is just like the dreamer's reaction *in the dream* you can suddenly see that your first dream-interpretation is already in the story! What happens because of it? In this way the dream-story can take you beyond your usual reaction.

Indian Chief Dream

A train stopped and a woman got off and came toward me. She said, "My baby is sick, can you help me?" We walked through this dark tunnel, for miles. Finally I heard a baby cry. We moved toward her, a little girl about 2 or 3, very pale....

Then there was an Indian man with feathers. I didn't understand a word he said to me. I felt there was no use communicating with him, as he wouldn't understand.

Then a woman dressed in white, with a very odd, threatening look, came toward me and I woke up.

First interpretation:

"That woman in white? Hospitals, nurses, death, something like that.

"The Indian looked great and wise, but not even he could understand me. I'm just isolated. Nobody would understand.

"The dream says something bad is coming. That's how it ends."

A second very different interpretation came when she used Question #5 summarizing the story for BIAS CONTROL, Part 2:

"First the Indian spoke to me. *Then I didn't understand, and I said he wouldn't understand me.* Only then did the woman in white come.

"Yes, that makes sense. When I say 'nobody would understand,' I'm angry but my anger turns on me and makes me hopeless. *Then* it feels like what that woman in white brings."

A dream often shows *you* acting in some puzzling way, which is actually a metaphor for how you do act, usually. It might be your way in relation to others, or toward a part of you. Include your way of acting in the story-summary. See what then happens as a result.

QUESTION #7 (WHAT PART OF YOU?) often adds a whole new view:

What part *of you* is this? (We have had examples of the big shift this question can make. See the Birthday Present Dream, Chapter 2.)

Check this: If you know that the bad thing is in fact in the situation or in an actual person, have you considered whether it might *also* be a suppressed part of you?

That wouldn't mean it wasn't *also* in the situation, of course.

For example, in your dream your spouse behaves as usual. Try considering *also* what part of you that might be. We often live with people who exemplify just what we suppress in ourselves. So it wouldn't be mysterious if this "bad" thing were both in that person and in you (although suppressed). Then it helps to see both.

Example: Ellen is thinking of leaving her husband, but is unsure about it. Now she dreams:

Basement Door Dream
I am in the basement with him, and the back door of the basement is open. Marge is standing outside. I run away from him and toward the outside, but then I wake up.

She says: "The dream shows I should leave him. Here I am in this dark hole with him, and the light is out there. Marge is divorced. I should join her. That's what it means."

Have you learned something new from the dream?

"Sure have. It seems to say I've got to get out of here, out of the dark."

Now the BIAS CONTROL: The opposite would be to stay with him. O.K., don't adopt that either. Now what?

Applying QUESTION #7 (WHAT PART OF YOU?):

"Well, that isn't me, that's him all right, very emotional, very intense, crowding me. He leaves me no space.

"But if that were also a suppressed part of me, what would that be in me? Hmm. In the basement where it's dark. Some part I don't see too well. Down far? Me emotional, intense, something I want to get away from?

"I don't know, nothing comes."

Something might have come there. In fact she did not get anything in the actual example. But the BIAS CONTROL can still protect her from falling entirely for her first interpretation. It can at least put that interpretation in doubt.

Check this: Did you make the dream take one side of a known conflict?

In general, a dream doesn't side with one side or the other of a conflict you know about, like staying or leaving. A dream will not say which you should do. *A dream brings up certain factors, and puts them into a story that can enable you to get beyond where you are stuck.* That may lead to a good decision.

The growth step isn't staying or leaving. She knows these action-possibilities already. *The growth step is a new way of bodily being,* which may lead to new actions too.

Life decisions are not up to the dream. But, someone might argue this way: Since the conscious self is incomplete without "the other side," isn't it right to obey the other side in the dream? If she feels like running out, doesn't it "prove" that the dream says she should stay? No indeed! The conscious self is incomplete, sure. But the other side is equally incomplete without your conscious attitudes and choices.

What you usually reject should not alone do your deciding for you, either.

The growth-step will be new. It probably isn't in the dream itself—the dream presents the constellation as it now is. The new step is neither of the present opposites.

QUESTION #8 (HOW WOULD YOU BE THAT PERSON?) was already taken up. It was the first way I mentioned under BIAS CONTROL, Part 2.

QUESTION #10 (SYMBOLS?):

Check this: Did you ignore what the dream-story said when you filled a meaning in for the object?

For example, in the Broken Vase Dream of Chapter 4, the dreamer felt that the vase she gave her mother stood for herself and it was "beautifully carved." But she interpreted that as: "Maybe it was beautiful before it broke, but not since then."

In another example, a woman dreamed of a beautiful, very large dolphin hidden in dark water. When she woke up, the image scared her! So she decided it was bad. But a dolphin is in a high order of living things! That needs to be filled into the dream: Some large, positive life force is still mostly hidden from her and it scares her.

QUESTION #12 (COUNTERFACTUAL?):

As in the Broken Vase Dream of Chapter 4, a whole section of the vase was broken out, and yet the liquid did not spill. But she interpreted the dream from the negative feeling she had about herself (both in the dream and about the dream) *so that she did not notice this at first.*

QUESTION #13 (CHILDHOOD?):

Sometimes we recall something from childhood but interpret the dream in a way that only repeats our reaction at that time. Then we need BIAS CONTROL.

Suppose you were mistreated in some way as a child. At the time you reacted as best a child could. Now you might be able to do more.

At the time the events might have been very discouraging. Don't settle for an interpretation that now discourages you in the same way!

For example, the dream leads to a memory of getting beaten in childhood. The dreamer might then feel: "I'll never get over it. I'll never be all right."

BIAS CONTROL asks: Is the interpretation itself an example of the old reaction? Wasn't that how the child reacted to the beating? It would be very understandable if the child had felt, "I'll never get over it. I'll never be all right." Of course, that deep feeling is still there and goes with the memory.

If the interpretation feels the way you felt then (beaten down, helpless, etc.), recognize it as belonging to that time. Then give that feeling
some space. Respect and comfort the child which did the best it could.
Every adult also has the child inside. *Be a friendly and caring adult with
the child that lives inside you.*

Then your interpretation doesn't just repeat the discouragement. You
permit that feeling to be there ("I'll never be all right") but that isn't
your interpretation of the dream. Rather, it becomes: "Oh, that hurt in
me needs my care and understanding. Back then I had to force everything
down. I couldn't survive otherwise. Well, now I can at least give it some
room."

There might also be other steps with that feeling, for example, getting to know it better, becoming able to bear it, understanding exactly
what happened, and so on.

Don't stop yet if the interpretation makes you feel as you felt in the
remembered events. What step comes for that feeling of then?

HAVE YOU USED
THE MOST IMAGINATIVE PART OF THE DREAM?

Dreams are marvelous in making up intricacies and situations you
could never have thought of. You can usually locate a part of a dream
about which you could say: "How odd! *That's* something I've never heard
of before."

So often it is just that part which our interpretation ignores.

Locate that part of your dream, and if you haven't used it in your
interpretation, do so.

THE BIAS CONTROL
MAY JUST TELL YOU TO GO ON WORKING

If your interpretation is not new, simply decide that you aren't
finished working when you thought you were.

There are always parts of any dream that remained uninterpreted,
and you can use all the questions about one of those parts.

*Especially if you have a negative interpretation—and especially if
that view of things is not new to you, don't stop with that.*

*Before you stop interpreting a dream, check your interpretation with
the BIAS CONTROL. What might be a growth-step in the seemingly negative direction? Then let your body give you the right quality.*

The Bias Control, Part 1
- Find the opposite interpretation but don't adopt that either

The Bias Control, Part 2
- Use the most imaginative part of the dream
- Use questions and checks in this chapter
- Then let your body-sense give you the step from the opposite

Chapter 11

Dream Symbols
and Metaphorical Language:
More on Question #10

Each person is unique. Therefore "universal" symbols cannot have the same meaning in everyone's dreams.

And yet a garden hose stands for a penis and woman's purse for a vagina.

How can we reconcile this contradiction?

Humans deal with many objects that have the same uses for us all. We walk with our feet, go fast in cars, stop with the brakes, use a comb to separate and straighten our hair. A purse is something you reach into, and women carry them. We all hold a garden hose so that the liquid spurts out in front of us.

Universal symbols are not an enemy's code designed to throw you off. Rather, human life gives most objects some universal functions and meanings.

Therefore, even without Freud, you can ask yourself, "What is a garden hose, anyway, and how is it used? One holds it sticking out in front of oneself above ground level, and a liquid spurts out of it, which makes the grass grow."

Especially if you use not only your mind but also the body-feel of standing there, using the hose, it will soon give you its universal meaning.

Now the other side of the question: Each individual is unique and lives a unique life. *The person's associations may change the object's usual meaning.* "Our garden hose is all tightly rolled up and has been left that way since we bought it. It came that way from the store and we've never used it."

Here the hose clearly stands for something left unused, tightly coiled, lying there ignored. Whether it mainly means that sexual power is left in this way remains to be seen. It is not certain. Perhaps the person

85

works in a hardware store or borrowed the hose from a difficult neighbor. Then it need not be a phallic symbol.

Nothing in a dream is *merely* the universal. It will always contain the unique and complex texture of this person, this life.

We all walk on feet, but your walking in your life is different from mine. The interesting part is the different part. No dream can be interpreted by universal symbols any more than I can know a lot about you because you have feet.

Every common thing is a symbol in that it brings a cluster of common uses, meanings, and functions. These provide a kind of graph paper, a background design, which helps us interpret the unique dream.

I will offer many examples. Take a look at each. Ask yourself what that thing is, anyway. Then you will see how to let any object suggest its universal meaning.

One can also ask (as with Question #7): If this object were part of the human personality, what part would it be? Everyone knows, of course, that clothes cover up the body. But we take a little turn, if we think of clothes as *a part of a person*. Clothes are people's "front," their "public identity," the way they present themselves.

An animal lives from instinct as nature intends it to live. Now think of that as part of a human person: that in us which would live instinctually as nature intends.

OBJECT	SUGGESTIVE SYMBOLIC MEANING
Animal	Instinctual aspect of person; natural life-energy
Animals, higher	Wise, healthy part of an organism; accept its guidance
Animals, other	What is the usual character of that animal? e.g., lions are proud, strong, kingly
Beach	Edge of conscious and unconscious; where the earth goes under water; where things emerge from the ocean
Car	Takes you somewhere; person moving, changing, going ahead; perhaps sexuality (who is driving? In what ways are you in process these days?)

Child	Vulnerable part, new self, growth process (If in your dream the child is 4 years old, ask yourself what began for you 4 years ago, or what happened when you were 4?)
Child, retarded	Undeveloped part of you; in what way have you been too afraid to live as you would have liked to live?
Clothes	Outer aspects; front; a person's public identity
Clothes, specific	That part of the body (sense tension in it?); ties—throat, crying, bonds to certain people; what does one do with that part of the body?
Clothes, whether they fit or not	Way of presenting yourself to others; your roles; body-feel, body-image; when you get fat or different, your old clothes don't fit; owning your body
Contraption, intricate machine, device	Person's functioning, perhaps body, sexual
Corset	Holding things in; rigid; female
Darkness	Unconscious; unseen; unaware
Doors, walls, windows	Something can or cannot come in, or out; defenses; you can look through the window, yet you aren't there
Eating	Taking in, making part of yourself
Explosion	Anger
Female stereotype	Receptive, emotional, moody, creative
Guard, gatekeeper	Keeps you or something out (or in); you may have to ask why or what
Hits you from the back or while you're asleep	Something catches you unawares

Ice	No feelings, anesthetic, cold
Indians	Primitive, close to nature, probably sound
Kitchen	Where you eat, get nourished and taken care of
Light	Lets you see what might have been in the dark; spiritual light
Male or female, unknown	Ancient stereotypic "male" or "female" sides of you; everyone has and needs both; if the opposite sex figure is in bad shape, negative, or attacking, check your *inward* relation to your own way of being the opposite sex's dimensions
Male stereotype	Directing, tackling reality, taking care of yourself, aggressive
Manager	Person in charge; take seriously; knows and is in charge of what goes on in this inner place; also: conductor, doctor, teacher, landlord, owner, guide, janitor
Movie, television	Presents story so you can see it as if not you
Ocean	Vast; can't see what's under water; unconscious
Old man, unknown	Wise guidance; an elder—listen to him; how do you treat him in the dream?
Old woman, unknown	Female wisdom; how to be a woman; what men don't grasp
Plane, flying, birds	Not being on the ground, skipping over obstacles; may mean being ungrounded; may have to be dealt with; being in one's head; perhaps also higher dimensions of the person

Plants, green	Living; life coming through in that spot
Policeman	Defends the public law
Roaches, bugs	Perfectly harmless creatures that disgust us; the rejected instinctual or body side of the person
Shoes	What you touch ground with; reality contact; you put them on when you go out into the world
Sleep	Unconscious; unaware; don't see
Telephone, radio	Message from unseen place, from unconscious
Tiger, shark	Aggressive instincts; integrate them; we need these; don't leave them separated off
Toilet	Problems left over from childhood toilet training may appear here; where you get rid of waste
Train	Process going on with you, in you, beyond your deliberate control. (Can you see where you're going? Can't get off once it starts? Compulsive? Could be growth process moving; we don't totally control that)

But how reliable are these translations?

They are unreliable! You can see that from the contradictory interpretations I sometimes gave to one symbol. A thing can have many uses. I will have omitted a lot of what each thing can be.

We would love to rely on such meanings to decode a dream, but your dream is not understood until your growth-step appears. These meanings are very helpful *to try out,* but not to adopt.

They are founded on just what that kind of thing is, in nature, in our society (and in this person's life).

Why are animals "good guides"? Because, in fact, animals live by instinct and fulfill their nature perfectly. They don't just "symbolize" the healthy organism, they *are* healthy organisms.

Why is a white-haired old man a good guide? Because one gets wiser when one gets older, and the very old have lived and seen a great deal. Just look at a painting of some unknown old man. Who wouldn't like an old man like that to show up in a crisis and tell us calmly what to do? That is the common meaning. (It can mean something else.) This old man might look like one the dreamer dealt with yesterday, perhaps a very different type of old man.

Why does a child symbolize growth process or new self? Because children *are* new and fresh, tender, the hope of humankind. They *are* new selves.

This method applies to anything. Ask yourself what that thing usually *is*. It may have a number of different natures. Rather than forcing one of these, sense each in turn, questioningly, to see what resonates with the dream. If nothing emerges directly, drop the supposed symbol meaning.

With other people's dreams, make sure they understand this questioning use. Ask: "Well, what's a comb, anyway? What would you say?" You can also add your own statement of what a comb is, but then say: "It might be. Just try it out. Does anything come?"

Or, preface it with: "Some people say a _____ can stand for _____ ." Make it clear that none of this is certain.

You are sensitively asking for something to pop in. If nothing does, let it go, as with the other questions.

For example, what *is* a comb? It is used for bodily cleanliness and care, but so is a toothbrush. (But that may be the point. The person who doesn't buy new combs probably uses a soggy toothbrush too.) What's special about a comb? It can have fine teeth...a fine-toothed comb... going through things with a fine-toothed comb.

Dirty Comb Dream:

They said some little boy was sick. He was in the house and I was outside with Janet. They asked me to come and help. I gave them my comb and told them to take it to the boy. Later he died but they said it wasn't my fault.

Associations: "The combs I have are cruddy but I haven't bought new ones. When I wash my hair I feel silly using dirty combs."

Here it's clear. The comb does mean body-care and investing care in oneself, even though a soggy toothbrush could have meant that as well. But we can also go on.

What is a comb? Something with fine teeth that separates the hairs. Careful discriminating, perhaps. Let's add that to what he said about combs.

Where in your life do you put the same old cruddy way on a new, fresh start? Where are you not making new distinctions, separating things out carefully, in perhaps a life-and-death matter?

What is a boy? A not-quite grown person, new growth, a new start, perhaps something that began about as many years ago as the boy is old.

How old was the boy? "Maybe four or five." What began four or five years ago? "Oh, of course, my new way. I know what it is!" Fill that into the dream: Am I putting the same old way on something new in me? Is there a way I don't give it enough energy and investment? Am I sort of letting it die?

Use symbols gently and questioningly, with a sense that a symbol might have meaning in a variety of directions. You are like a blind person tapping in the dark.

A regular dictionary can give you the common characteristics of something you don't know well. There are also dictionaries of symbols. These can be extremely useful. But be on guard:

We are beyond the simple-minded notion that you could look your dream up in a dream dictionary. A symbol is a complexity pictured in a metaphor, as in a poem. It does not equal a phrased or defined meaning.

A good poet would not look symbols up in an old collection (for example, look up "discouragement" and find "gray sky"). Good poems have fresh, unique images.

Neither does the dream-making in you just look up "same old way of doing things" in a dictionary and find there the suggestion "dirty comb." It finds that in the person's unique life, in how that person deals with combs.

But it helps to think also what a comb's primary function is. It is for cleanliness, tidiness, and it can be fine-toothed. Let the universal notion and its feel-quality resonate with the dream and the associations.

Here are some short examples, small dream-bits, to accustom you to the metaphoric language of dreams. You don't know the whole dream nor the associations. Therefore you can *conclude* nothing. The things and the bit of story can give you a general sense for the *kind* of thing it *might* mean. Such a general sense helps in working with a dream. You would let your associations and what comes in you modify and change such a general sense.

To give you some practice, I tell my versions afterwards. First ask yourself: As a universal way of speaking, what might this story say?

1. I was lying in a room off the kitchen with no door.

2. Our house was swept clean, not a bit of clutter anywhere. All the chairs were covered with muslin dust covers, like a summer home readied for the owners to leave.

3. I put some of the flowers in a cheap little glass that I have kept to use as a vase, but the top is too narrow, so I transfer them to a similar one with a wider top, which is perfect.

4. Just as I had gotten on the bus and paid, I saw my grandmother walking toward another bus. I immediately got off my bus and boarded hers.

5. I became mesmerized by the beautiful, vast, enormous snow-capped mountains appearing from the clouds.

6. There was an old granite building. The stone work looked very strong. The building appears to have withstood a great deal of harsh weather without any visible signs of damage. I feel a strong desire to explore the interior of this building.

7. Two girls were putting a cast on my leg. Then they said I needed a full body cast. I jumped up and started shouting. The doctor came and ordered them out.

8. There was a line of sheep waiting to get through several gates. I was helping them through, and I hugged this one black sheep with my whole body.

9. My brothers got very mean and took all the buttons off the phone and the doorknobs off the doors.

10. My father was building something and teaching me about it and my feet were naked and I am getting dirt and grease all over them and it's squooshy.

11. Dick and I had our cars linked together. We were in the one in back. The cars were going backwards so fast I had to brake hard to stop them.

12. My parents were going to that crater in Hawaii. I emphasized to them that they must go all the way down to the bottom and through it.

13. Sharon let a bull into the stable where I was, and the bull charged me. I was real angry and I climbed up the wall to protect myself. I didn't get hurt. Instead I ended up in the next room where there was a banquet.

14. I pulled out a very underdeveloped baby from my body. The baby was perfectly formed but I pulled it out of the womb too soon.

15. I was cooking two babies in a stew. My mother said she was

given a psychological test that showed she was strong enough to handle the situation. Then I was taking care of a strong baby.

16. My grandmother said, "Now I can give you all my money," and her money was under her head in her pillow and she pulled it out.

17. I'm up on a bridge but it stops in the air. I have to go down and get across a lot of mud. I follow some track and get across.

18. Jenny [her baby] has a big shit. As I clean it up it's also mixed with my shit, and there is more and more of it. I can't clean it all up. Then a girl comes, with dark, curly hair. She has a sore on her leg. She says she doesn't mind the shit, it might even heal her sore.

POSSIBLE METAPHORICAL MEANINGS

Yours may differ from mine and be just as right. Add mine and let them expand your "general sense," which you would try out.

1. *Kitchen*—cooking, food, nourishment, taking something in; what is a kitchen? what goes on there?
   No door—open to whomever, defenseless, no control? What is a door?
   Lying down—Defenseless, passive? Childhood experience with kitchen, with taking in, with lying down? Maybe open to what's cooking, to being nourished?

2. *Leaving some place*—too clean, not usable, not actually living in it? Is something so protected from dirt that it can't be lived in? Something is being put away for safekeeping?

3. *Cheap little glass*—not enough energy or care for this? Or, it looks cheap, but it's perfect
   Flowers—something living and beautiful
   A vase—the female sex organ? A little more room to put something living in? Something long kept and not used?

4. *Bus*—takes you to some destination. You aren't now going your own way, having your own destination?
   Grandmother—You're now living some traditional way, an old way? Or is it wise and better first to go that old woman's way?

5. *Vast, high mountains, beautiful*—spiritual, cosmically meaningful,

big opening, large vision? What comes just before this? How did you get there? What is associated with this? Whatever this stands for is of great value. In the clouds, perhaps not quite grounded yet?

6. *Building*—perhaps you. You've gone through a lot, withstood a lot?
   No visible damage—it doesn't show?
   Desire to explore—explore the inside of it, your own inwardness?

7. *Cast—part or all of your body could be made rigid.* No feelings there where the cast holds it in?
   Doctor—a wiser part of you throws out what makes you rigid. (Can you sense something in you that would throw them out? Be that a while.)
   Girls—make you "rigid"? Erection? Tense? A female part of you? A young part of you?

8. *Sheep*—warm, good animal side of you.
   Black sheep—it has been disapproved of in the past
   Gate—it's coming through what used to be a barrier?

9. *Telephone*—you hear from unseen source, from the unconscious?
   No buttons, no knobs—isolation, can't communicate, can't go out
   Brothers—childhood abuse? Good brothers? Keep you in this spot for your own good? Part of you isolates you?

10. *Father, building something, teaching me*—good father roles
    Getting feet dirty—in earth, real stuff
    Squooshy—sexual, mucous, sense of body and earth

11. *Cars*—going somewhere. Maybe physical, sexual being.
    Backwards—sliding back, to where you've been? Going back? Perhaps something with your backside?

12. *Crater*—deep into the earth, unconscious, deep down
    Volcanic crater—anger, explosiveness
    Parents—related to the origin of some of your personality; your childhood. Their problem is in you some way.
    To the bottom—get to the bottom of it (the dreamer, added, "especially about the trouble between them"). Face it. Trouble in the ground; something stands in the way of getting grounded.

13. *Bull*—sound animal instinct, can be strong
    The bull charged...I was angry—anger; some of it is still coming at you? Is something out of control in your life?
    Climbed the wall—You take care of yourself, protect yourself? Had more feelings than you could stand ("climbing the walls")? At first it seemed too much for you? You tried to climb the walls to get away from it?
    Banquet—eating, taking in, digesting, integrating, nourishing, expanding. So it seemed too much for you, but afterwards you made it part of you and you felt larger. Does that fit?

14. *Baby*—new life, vulnerable, new development
    I pulled it out—are you doing something, insisting you should be further along than you quite are?
    Womb—vagina, sexual, creative spot where something is developing
    Too soon—it's developing perfectly, but it's too soon now to take it out

15. *Stew*—something eventually eaten, taken in, integrated; a unity of many things cooked (processed) so they go together
    Two babies—two still vulnerable, very new developments
    Strong baby—strong new way of being
    Psychological test—something wise and knowing says... (only in dreams are psychological tests to be taken that way!)
    Mother—Your actual mother is strong enough to stand it. (When you were little, did you have to take care of her?) The part of you that is your mother is strong enough to stand it.

16. *Money*—value, energy, power. What did your grandmother have that's of value? What was she like?
    Her *head*—thinking? insight? concentration? will power?
    Under her head—she kept it safe and out of sight with her head, but not in her head
    Now I can give you—What did she have that you're only just now ready for?

17. *Bridge*—way to get across
    Mid-air—up high, thinking, not grounded, skipping over
    Mud—earth, concrete reality, muddy, unclear, slow going. You wish you could skip over a lot, but you might have to go through it.

Feelings? Actual experience? It's muddy, earthy, the ground, feet
on the ground. Seems there is some track to follow and you do
get through O.K. What are you hesitant about getting into in your
own development now? Perhaps the dream says you can actually
go through it.

18. *Baby*—new life, new development, your actual baby and your growth
   Shit—natural stuff, organic bodily matter, left over from digestion
   Clean it up—eliminate smelly, earthy stuff. You think it is shit and
      has to be cleaned up but, actually, it can heal something?
   Girl—the sensitive, receptive, emotional part. It can heal that part
      of you? Healing her has to do with your new development, perhaps
      also with Jenny.

Of course we need the whole dream, the associations, and what the
questions would bring. Without these we cannot know whether such symbolic meanings apply. Sometimes we can think of opposite possibilities.
But the symbols and metaphors do give us something to ask about.

III

The Continuing Process

Chapter 12

How To Continue the Growth Process

KNOWING YOUR GROWTH PROCESS
AND BRINGING IT BACK WHEN IT'S LOST

Perhaps you are changing and developing as a person. Then you know the good energy of that sense of movement which is more than you can conceptualize. There is a lot of struggle. Sometimes you don't do well or get far. There are times when you get discouraged and it feels bad. *But then you remember:* "Hey, I've lost track of my good growth process! Where is it?"

Just recalling it may bring it back somewhat. The fact that we often lose it is no surprise. "I fell off. I want to get back on."

There are many ways to bring it back. One way is by use of the dream images. Physically sensing or being one of them can let the good new edge come again, livingly, physically. "Ah...it's so much better to be alive and growing than that other way I felt.

It's true, one cannot always renew the sense of forward movement just like that. Even when not, it helps to know what a *continuing growth process* feels like and to look for it. Do you know what it is like so that you can look for it?

Don't let your dream-interpreting remain a brilliant shot now and then, without a continuing process.

Sense the message from a dream as a step on your long-term growth-line. If the dream brought you a bit of new bodily being, can you live in that way in some situation today? Perhaps choose a less important situation in which to practice. Can you be that new way inside? Can you also be curious about what might get in the way? Let the change-direction be tentative, and look to see what further steps come in your body.

All this has a continuity from day to day, like world news or the National League.

Once a continuing growth process takes off, it is bigger than what we can understand or do deliberately. It is much more than focusing, but focusing helps it start and continue.

FOCUSING

When the process seems lost and gone, you recall its feel-quality and that helps bring it back. Remembering that good energy, you sense your body's heavy refusal to feel that good way. No. It resists. *That* heavy resistance which is in the way, focus on *that*.

What is in the way is often interesting. It becomes more interesting when listened to, because it goes through steps. Whatever is in the way— focus on *that*. Sense it directly *as a physically felt "can't"* ("don't want to," "dare not," etc.)

Words run on: "I couldn't do it, Jim wouldn't like it and I can't leave him 'cause I'm too weak and dependent and I hate myself and...." Stop and focus on *that* bodily sense of "I couldn't...."

Suppose what is in the way is that you don't feel like focusing—aha, focus on that sense of not wanting to focus. Wonder what's in *that*.

Some current methods concentrate on wonderful altered state experiences, unbelievable terror or wonder flooding the person. I know these can be valuable. But all who work with this type of experience agree that one needs times of "integration" afterwards. The floods themselves don't provide the "integration." That word stands for *you growing,* rather than for your being a passive spectator of great experiences. The small person that survives these big experiences can be more brittle than ever. I am not speaking against such experiences but of the need for focusing.

Other methods concentrate on intense emotions, as if by expressing them you could press them all out of you. But they don't leave, one makes them over and over again. One needs to sense under them, where they are made.

I am not speaking against emotions. When they come, let them through. Don't block them. Welcome them. Welcome crying and anger. Be gentle with sadness. But intense emotions often repeat. If you don't block them, you will find the deeper, wider level of the felt sense. (Or, if you have to block them, focus on the body-sense of not wanting them.) That will get you to a new edge.

New edges are rarely intense emotions. Usually they don't grab us and refuse to let go, as emotions do. It is often difficult to keep hold of the growth direction. Our old mode of being is more intense and quickly closes a new opening. The felt sense that brings the new opening is not as intense. It is not familiar like anger, fear, hate, sadness, or joy. At first there are not even words for it.

YOU NEED A PARTNER

It is much more possible to go deeply into yourself when another person gives you quiet attention. Of course you focus mostly alone. But it helps greatly to meet with someone weekly or more often. Split the time, half for you, half for the other. Do as you need in your time and let the other person do whatever they need in the other half.

Try it for an hour or two with one person and then with another, until you have found someone with whom you want to continue.

You need not only focus and work on dreams. The time is for you. You use it as you wish.

YOUR GROWTH PROCESS
DOESN'T DEPEND ON ANY EXPERT

Many current methods depend on some wonder-worker who does things to you. You have big experiences, but not *your* continuing growth process. That person makes the experiences from outside you, into you. They are single shots, no process. No need to refuse if you know such a person, but then use the experiences as you would dream break-throughs—sense your way toward *a continuing process of yours*.

The kind of steps you get from focusing and dreams are indeed the sort that come in deep psychotherapy. But therapy includes a continuing special relationship, and hours of going deeply inside.

The next set of chapters offers a number of ways dreams can help continue your process.

Chapter 13

Are You Really Doing It?
Six Ways To Check Yourself

Exactly how can we work in that *bodily* way I have mentioned? How can we get that *bodily* change, something sensed concretely, a new energy coming forward?

I am worried that you might take it all into your mind only and miss the whole point. Sensing your body cannot be written down here, it is for you to do, livingly, inside. It takes only minutes, and it feels good and life-enhancing. It is more of *you,* when it comes, and not what I make up or write here.

Here are some ways you can check if you are *really* sensing in a bodily way.

1. FIRST CHECK:
CAN YOU FEEL THE MIDDLE OF YOUR BODY?

Let me ask you to shift your attention to the inside of your stomach. Are you instantly there? Do you sense some fuzzy, woolly feel, or perhaps some tightness there?

Roughly two-thirds of people can instantly do that. About a third cannot. They can feel the periphery of their bodies, arms, legs, head, back, but not the middle inside.

We can now teach this to almost everyone who cannot do it at first.

Begin by finding one of your big toes without moving it. If you cannot find it, move it a little—there it is. Now stop moving it, and notice that you are now in your toe. That's what it's like. Think about something else, and then see if you can find your toe from inside, without moving it. Whether you can or not, go on:

Do the same with your knee. Can you find it? If not, flex slightly

103

—there it is. Go on up to your groin, and then into your stomach. Are you there? Is it nice and woolly in there, or tight and heavy? Or how?

If this is hard for you, practice it during the day, between things, and very soon it will be easy. It needs to become easy in order to focus.

2. SECOND CHECK: CAN YOU SENSE THE UNCLEAR?

If you can sense what you don't know, then you are focusing. You don't know what it is, yet there it is. It has a life of its own. If you try to define it, it refuses and denies what you thought. If you keep your attention on a felt sense for some moments, it will do something. You needn't. Just let it. Merely stay by it. If you lose it, come back to it. Keep it company. Ask it questions.

Does your felt sense have such a life of its own?

Most people don't know about the felt sense yet. They may have had one at rare times. For example, sometimes one has a hunch that something is wrong even though nothing seems wrong. Logically some situation seems just fine and yet there is this odd and unclear sense. One tries to argue it away, but it has a life of its own, and stays. After it opens and releases, something important may then become clear. A hunch is a kind of felt sense. But hunches are rare.

Focusing is a way of letting your body give you something like a hunch, whenever you want one. Only now we wouldn't call it a "hunch" because that word has a more specific meaning. We call it a felt sense.

At first it seems very unpromising, next to nothing. You may say, "What? This? This murky, unsatisfyingly vague, queasy, confused feeling? Are you telling me something will come out of *this?*" Yes. That's just what I'm saying. You're attending in the right place.

3. THIRD CHECK: WHEN MEMORIES OR NEW IMAGES COME, CAN YOU LET THEM LEAD YOU TO THE BODY-SENSE WHICH COMES WITH THEM?

For example: In Question #8 (How would you be that person?), words and moves to do on stage might come to you, spontaneously. Can you go to their source in your body, that *body-sense* from which they came? You want not only words and moves but that bodily way of being as well.

Words or images may suddenly come. They are intriguing, but can you contact their source in your body? If tears come, can you sense the crying in you?

Focusing is attending directly in that "edge," that "zone" between conscious and unconscious. Directly. That means physically, sensing *that, there*. You will experience new energy and a change coming, *there*.

4. FOURTH CHECK: CAN YOU STAY, OR CAN YOU RETURN OVER AND OVER?

Now I worry that you may quit a minute too soon. You may find all I describe but not stay the extra little time it needs. A felt shift or a new energy needs a whole minute or two. I have said this before but now that you have read this far, I must say it again. It may make the difference between getting real personal development or not.

You can decide if you know what I mean: If you do, you will agree that staying with something is difficult. Before the shift comes, one has trouble staying because the felt sense is so murky. Right after it opens and shifts, it is wonderful, and yet then, too, somehow we say: "O.K. I've got it, it's great, yes, that's the new way I need to be. I need it like life itself. I've had it for three seconds, let's stop."

How does one "stay with" a felt shift or return to it?

Notice your desire to stop, you let that through. You take a moment's breather. Then see if you can find the new energy again. What was it? Oh, yes, you remember. Is it here now? No. Can you get it back by willing it back? No. But it was here only moments ago. Yes, but it isn't here now.

It only just came, and went away almost as fast? That moment alone has not changed you very much. That is why this chapter may make the difference. How can you bring the felt shift back so that you can stay with it?

You repeat whatever you did just before it came. What were you doing then? Attending in your body. Now you go back down there. What were you asking then? Oh yes. Now you ask that again. Oh, and then you had that image, and then .... ah, there it is again, that felt shift!

This applies also to working with other people's dreams. What I presented so far may seem elegant. You ask some questions, restate them in various ways, and everything opens up. You can be effective, poised; you seem powerful and competent. Others are amazed at your capacity. But to help someone process a dream *really*, you may have to give up on elegance.

When the interpretation seems complete, the dream has given its new edge, you see *what a great change it would be if the person could really have this change!* But that isn't likely from the first brief moment. Now it is hard and messy to get the person to recontact the new energy and keep it for a few more moments. Not everyone is willing to go over what just happened, to arrive again at the shift.

Of course, if it did not feel good, drop it. But if it is as I have described, then we may have to urge the person to spend another minute having it again.

After that, can the person keep the shift so it can be recontacted at different times that day? "Do you feel you could get it back, any time you want?" From the tone of voice in the answer you can recognize if it is possible as yet. If not, it helps to ask, "Why does that seem hard to do? Can you sense what is in the way?"

Getting another person to do this is often impossible, especially since the overriding purpose is to let the person enjoy the dream (the last "How-To" point). And, certainly, all this need not happen the first few times you work with someone. It takes many times.

But with your own dreams, do you return and let the new energy come over and over again, for some minutes?

5. FIFTH CHECK:
DOES YOUR BODY KNOW IT CAN EXPRESS ITSELF?

To keep a felt shift, and live from it, the body may need to move in some expressive way. How would your body move and be if this new way were how you live? Let that new person emerge. For example, your elbows may want to expand in a way that makes room for you. Your chest may want to inhale, or relax, or whatever comes from this new quality. Or, you find yourself strutting around, sensing yourself stronger, "Come on, anybody, just give me trouble, see what happens, I'm ready."

Most people rarely live in their bodies. You may need to let your body know that it is allowed to come up with such expressive moves.

To give your body expressive permission, practice a little without focusing on anything. Exhale and let your shoulders and whole body loose. Pretend something is very strengthening: square your shoulders, ready for any trouble. Pretend something is vastly expansive, like a big mountain scene: inhale and feel your chest as big as the scene. After that your body knows it can express itself. When real feelings come, it is free to express them in its own way.

When you get a felt shift, your body will give you its unique expression without your prompting.

6. SIXTH CHECK:
DO YOU "PRACTICE" WITH SMALL ACTION STEPS?

A real change involves not only acting differently in some situations. It is a change in how you are alive, in the *manner of experiencing*. In the long run that changes all the situations in ways you cannot plan in advance.

Becoming able to live in a new manner is like developing a muscle. You stretch it a little, then you stretch it again; you work bit by bit. Usually you cannot live in accord with a new energy all at once. But you can recall the image and privately feel the new body quality many times during a day. You can also continue that into actions.

There is a way of action which doesn't count as heavily as changing one's whole life immediately. We call it "practice."

When we "practice" something, we know we aren't doing it well— yet. There is room to fail, to fall down, and yet we give ourselves credit: We're actually practicing!

Choose some not-so-important situations, and try living from your new bodily quality. Design some at-first tiny steps.

Do you practice in action?

Chapters 15 and 16 tell more about how to do that. So far I have emphasized your development rather than specific situations. Now we will discuss these.

Chapter 14

Dreams Are Often Comments on the Momentary Condition of a Situation

A dream can *help* you to make a decision, it does not make it for you. Among other reasons, dreams are often reactions to what happened just the day before. Consider the following example:

Their marriage seemed to be on the rocks. They were all but separated and spent most of the time talking about it. In some of the talking that day Nancy got a small insight into herself. Then she dreamed:

Female Message Dream
Someone led me to the edge of a lake. Out of it came a woman who was also me. I was told that I would be female so I could be with him [her husband].

Could any sign be more definite? The dream says the trouble has been her incomplete femininity, and now it will fully arise and make their marriage possible. Obviously, she should stay. But don't conclude that so quickly.

She told the dream to her husband, and though he was glad, he maintained his argumentative attitude. He wanted her to see this and that point of his, and this argument led to more arguments. The next night she dreamed:

Watch-Her-Die Dream
He [her husband] has kidnapped and killed this woman, a very buxom, healthy woman, and he is sitting by the side of a deep well, just watching her, day after day, as she dies and disintegrates.

This dream, one night later, is equally indicative in the other direction. Clearly her husband is hostile to her femininity and she must get away from him.

The dreamer experienced both her dreams as comments on the previous day's interaction with her husband. These dreams make most sense
that way. Nancy's insight on the first day need not have remained as
small as it seemed. Her dream showed that her femininity had moved,
or could move, on a deep level in her. It was a fitting response to their
interaction that day. When he failed the next day to welcome her reaching
out to him, she then dreamed that he was letting this new feminine in
her die; he was not moving toward it; he was just sitting there watching.

Since dreams are so often momentary reactions, they cannot be taken
as indicating what ought to be done. See if your dream can be understood
as a barometer reading, a report, a comment on what occurred the previous day—as if to say: This is the latest change. This is where it is at
right now. *If* it keeps going this way, here's what would happen.

Or we could phrase it this way: Here is what needs a step, *just now,*
because of yesterday.

I don't say dreams always change like that. But often.

In this example the husband also had dreams that commented on
that bad day.

Dead Bird Dream
Down on the floor, next to a chair, was a brown paper bag with
a dead pigeon in it. I said they ought to put it in the cooler, not
leave it lying around in the hot room.

He added: "When I woke I realized the bird was my love for Nancy,
and it was dead, the dream said. I felt awful about it. In my chest it
felt like a bird fluttering, hurt. So it was still alive! The result was I felt
actually more hopeful afterwards."

What did you think, feel, and do yesterday, especially in your process with Nancy?

"We had a bad day. I went all day saying that it was over and I
ought to move out. I even wanted to move out yesterday, I kept hearing
it tell me in my mind the sooner the better. I forgot all about loving her."

The dream helped him see his own cold attitude toward his own
love feelings. ("The sooner, the better.") In the dream he says coldly,
in effect: "So it's dead. Don't let it lie here and smell."

His dream can be taken as a comment on yesterday. Then it also
brings more: He alternates between love and cold anger. Therefore, what
the dream pictures is not just yesterday. It can help him see and work
on that cold anger. But it must not be taken as a decision-indicative
message.

His *first reaction to the dream* was similar to his reaction in the dream: "My love for Nancy is dead." But then his further feelings led to a step in the opposite direction. The dream of the dead bird led to the physical coming of the living bird. This brings home how a dream's meaning should not be decided without the body.

In this example you can also see a special problem when people who live together tell each other their dreams. The effect can make a warning dream come true or defeat what it proposes. Or the other person's reaction can make a positive dream-possibility happen. The other person can hear a negative dream as a warning and react in a better way than the dream projects.

So, if you are both dreamed about and told the dreams, you can prepare yourself not to respond as the dream fears you will. Equally, you can prepare yourself to respond in accord with a good step a dream may suggest for you.

In telling your dream: If you know that your person will react negatively without preparation, a little work might be needed in advance of telling it.

Without this realization we often bring about just what the dream warned might happen.

Here is a rare perfect example:

"In one part of my dream I dreamed that I told him my dream and he got mad and that spoiled everything."

Did you tell him the dream?

"Yes, and he did get all upset. Since then we haven't been O.K. at all."

The example is unusual because it is so literal. More often a metaphorical story shows how the next interaction *might* be unfortunate. Then when you tell that person the dream, the reaction is often just what the dream projected. In such instances the dreamer should process the dream and experience a bit of positive change, growth, resolution before interacting with the person. Then, also, that person should be asked for the positive opposite which is lacking in the dream and be helped to find and have it. That may take a little work. Without it the person is likely to react from earlier bad feelings which the dream's negative image is likely to re-stimulate.

Let us not be passive toward dreams. We may long for an oracle with perfect knowledge. Developing is harder. The dream doesn't know if you will develop or not. If you do, that would change what the right action is. It might bring different alternatives. Therefore the dream does not know or say which of your current choices is right in the situation.

Human life is so arranged that there is no substitute for our struggles. They make us human in depth. Instructions for handling situations would improve only our performance. Our lives would look better but we would stay at the level we have already attained. If we could get right instructions, few would choose struggle instead. But there is no choice about that. We do not get situational guidance.

On the other hand, if we ask for development-steps, then there is guidance! Finely tuned little steps come.

We sense this guidance only when we become quiet inside, which is hard to do.

Moving one's attention there is deliberate. Once we sense the murky edge, we have to wait for the little steps. A certain queasy quality lets us know that something new is happening. Development must happen before it can be understood or pictured.

That is why the growth-step is often not pictured in the dream. Until more development, it cannot form. The dream pictures why it does not form, how things are stuck. Only processing the dream reveals the step.

When we take the step, *then* we say the dream brought it. Did we read it into the dream? No, the step came out of the dream, and yet it was not pictured. *Was* it there? Yes, but in an odd sense of the word "was." The step was not there as such, until the person takes it. Then, looking back, the dream is the best way to symbolize and remember the step. So it *was* there! The dream's symbols and figures were exactly what makes the step. As you re-picture the dream, the step comes again. The dream is the present constellation, but with an incipient change-step in it. That change may not have been pictured in the dream.

That is why the feel of a growth process is needed to get the dream's growth-step. Similarly, the right act in a situation is not usually in the dream itself.

Chapter 15

Helping You with People and Situations

If a dream (or its day residue) is about a specific situation, there is one more way to interpret it.

Take an example of an association: "Oh, yesterday I told Marcia about Bob."

Your situation with Marcia (any situation) is an intricate pattern. It's not just mentioning Bob to Marcia. You recall exactly what you said. It came just after a certain remark of hers. It came after your whole history with her. You recall why you said it, in what connection, what you both felt. You mentioned Bob because he is your friend and might help her get a job. How you were is one of your ways of being. You were trying to impress her with the range of people you know. Or you let her know you have other friends than her. Or you were trying to help, and carelessly got yourself into having to call Bob for a favor, although you haven't talked to him in years.

A situation is a very intricate pattern. The dream is also an intricate pattern. Each can help interpret the other. There are two ways to go:

1. We can use the situational pattern *to interpret the dream.*

Up to now in this book we took the dream as more deeply about you. We considered Marcia (in the dream or the associations) as a figure in a deep story about you. We used your situation with Marcia to interpret the dream about some issue of yours in many situations, not just with her.

2. Or we can use the dream *to interpret the situation.*

Now we move the other, or second, way as well. Let us now be interested in the situation for its own sake. What do we discover about it if we apply the dream and the answers to the questions? The metaphorical dream-story can highlight some aspects of the situation and how you act in it.

For example, see the dream in Chapter 11 about a dirty comb. The dream led to something deep about the dreamer. But what about the combs? Shouldn't he take the trouble to wash them or buy new ones? It may seem a superficial question. We took the comb *only* as a symbol the dream used. But he did say he uses dirty combs and doesn't buy new ones.

The dream points directly to an action step! Buy new combs or take the time to wash the old ones. Of course, that action would be only a small step on a general problem. But the dream points to small action steps he might not otherwise have thought of.

This may seem a tiny step when compared with the whole regime this dreamer might need.

This step may seem too tiny. If you had this dream, you would want a whole new regime of bodily care. But check back later. However tiny the step was, I bet you didn't actually manage to buy or wash the combs.

As you will see if you try them, small action steps have a lot of power. They are hard to do. They let you encounter and work through what is in your way. They change you. By the time you have done many small actions, you find you can do the large ones you could not do before.

Large and small action steps involve the same "aspect of life" the same "part of you" and "way of being." The deeper significance is implicit in the small action.

Therefore that man may have quite a struggle before he actually buys new combs. He can encounter and generalize what he meets in doing that.

The dream points to many action steps.

Buying new combs, the little action step, can be generalized as a big issue about body-care and taking care of himself. That can generate many other small action steps. Only action ultimately resolves most problems. Therefore action steps are needed as an integral part of what dreams mean. How hard the actions are can give you the best sense what was in the way. And only in actions does your body get to live the new way for more than a few symbolic moments!

For example, suppose your dream about Bob lead you to a more resilient bodily way of being. If you were this bodily way, you would never offer anything you don't really want to do. For a beautiful breakthrough minute you *are* like that. You decide to re-contact this feeling later today, and at every long red light as you drive home. But how could the situation with Marica give you an *action step?*

Let's see. You promised Marcia you would call Bob to tell him about Marcia's project and urge him to come to her meeting. It isn't how you want to renew your long-dormant relation with Bob. You wish you had not mentioned Bob, whom she knows. She could call him herself. You feel you "should not" have offered.

Now you will probably tend to miss the small action step here and go only for the big change: "Never again! I'll stop doing things for everyone at work, at home, and from now on. After calling Bob I will never again do things like that. I'm a different person. I will stare every demanding person down, and do only what I feel right about." Fine, if possible. But that huge change is unlikely. You can see how unlikely it is, if you try for a small action instead.

What would be a *small* action from that new body-feel? Well, the obvious one here would be with Marcia! You could call Marcia and tell her that, on second thought, you won't call Bob.

Now you probably feel: "Oh, no, never, I couldn't possibly! She was so glad that I would call him."

The new person was going to change everything. Now, in this tiny, perfectly possible step you encounter what keeps you as you are. But such tiny action steps *are* possible! It is therefore vital to struggle for a tiny step of that sort. Recontact the dream's new way of bodily being. From *that,* what would you now do with Marcia? ..... Sure, now you can call her.

You can take the action step especially if you think of it as "practice." If something is new for us, we cannot possibly expect ourselves to be good at it. You know you might not do the small action smoothly. It might even be a small disaster—but you will have done your practicing, you will be on the way!

First, interpret the dream broadly and internally. If it is understood deeply and brings a physical growth-step, it will also speak more clearly about this specific situation. The small action steps come best, later. But, either can help the other.

Let the dream give you a small action step in the very situation that is associated with it. Also look for small steps in other situations.

Action steps are vital. I devote the next few chapters to them.

Chapter 16

Finding Small Action Steps

We just saw how small action steps can be found in the situation from the dream (or in an associated situation).

Here are two more ways to find small action steps that let you practice the bodily manner of the felt shift from the dream.

SUBDIVIDED STEPS

Think of the smallest possible action step in the direction you want. Divide it into still smaller part-steps that may seem silly alone.

For example, dating. You should get out more, approach people, get dates. Fine, but that's the big action. What is a small step? Going once to a place where you might meet someone. Now subdivide that. It consists of getting there, going in, saying hello to someone, talking, arranging a date. So the first subdivision is getting there. It seems to make no sense, but you would be on your way if you *practiced* nothing but getting there for a while. Yes, it seems silly. You would set aside Friday night, drum up the energy, get dressed up, go to a place where you might meet someone, and when you're at the door, go home. Having done that ten times, you will see that it gets easy. Then practice going in, looking around for a minute, then going home. Now comes my favorite step: You get there, look around, and say hello to one person. Then you immediately turn on your heels and go home. It seems silly, but just that much turns out to be possible. You do this over and over in many places. After a while you can do five a night. By the time that gets easy, you have broken most of the inhibiting habits. Amazingly, the next steps become possible too.

When you have done the step you set yourself, *celebrate!* You have done your practicing!

117

The celebration is vital. Most people punish themselves if they even ever do try a small step, because it didn't bring the whole result they need. They try once and get depressed. It makes such steps harder in the future. If you did the step, be pleased about it. Reward your body with a good feeling. Celebrate—you are on the way!

Later decide on the next step. Again it must be small enough, so you *know* you can do it. It takes many weeks. But staying stuck takes years.

PRIVATE STEPS

One man's felt shift from a dream had a bodily quality something like a strong calm sense of, "You can't ride over me!"

Now he said, "I ought to confront that fellow, the one I have to deal with at work. I could get other people to come with me, and when he starts brow-beating me, I ought to say calmly, 'That's enough' or 'What is bothering *you* today, that you act like that?' But I can't do it."

That step is too big. Now, in addition to dividing and subdividing that step, there is another way: small private actions.

In this and other situations he can look for a tiny step that would still have *that bodily quality.*

What does he imagine doing in less important situations, if he were there with this new body quality? He imaged them, one after another. Many opportunities to practice arose. In one situation he thought of calling a halt to some bad treatment. With another person, a nonstop talker, he could at least interrupt. He might not know what to say, but he could cough. He remembered needing to go to the bathroom and waiting for a pause or a break. He then decided to begin with that person, and then others, with this "practice": Getting up immediately and going to the bathroom, no matter who is still talking.

This action step is small and private. No one knew he was doing something special. No one could stop him from doing it. And, yet, he practiced the new bodily quality he called, "You can't ride over me."

Again, you need to celebrate if you have lived in your new, right manner, however small the step. Take a minute just to say "Hurrah!" to yourself. Some concrete reward can also help.

Such little steps break the ice and move you ahead. They give you lots of energy.

Action can change the whole organism. A change in the organism changes how one acts. Work both ways.

Chapter 17

Progress in Dreams

When you make progress along a growth-dimension, your dreams usually report it. (Then, of course, you need not reverse it with the BIAS CONTROL.)

Take this dream, for example.

Book Award Dream
Riley (whom I know) had gotten an award for his book. It was the day after. We were at the agency that gave him the award. The girl behind the desk gave him back the copy of his book, a big, red volume. I made a joke about it. I said to Riley, "So they're not really giving you anything, just your own book back." Riley wheeled around and said, "Come on, don't you think it's a nice award?" I instantly realized I was being envious, so I said very firmly and strongly, "Yes, it really is. I'd like to talk to you." He looked at me and changed his attitude immediately. He thought a minute: "Will you be on the train?" I said yes, I would be. He said, very positively, "All right. See you on the train."

Associations: "Riley is a very negative person, everyone agrees about that. He's very nasty to most people. But in my dream he does an impressive job cutting through my negative attitude. But I did meet him straight on, too. I turned right around. I admire *this* Riley in the dream and also my turning right around. But ..... umm, in reality I couldn't do that yet. I am heading that way, though! Yes, the part of me that is like *this* is getting much more positive as I get more positive, straight, and meet things head-on. It feels good. *I'm making progress!*"

Here Dan knows the direction of his recent growth, and the dream reports his progress and moves a little further ahead. ("But, umm, in reality I couldn't do that yet.")

Dan doesn't need to try out the opposite here, it would be his old way. Becoming more positive and confronting is his growth edge, and he recognizes it in the dream. Both the Dream-Riley and he exemplify that direction.

This is an example of dreams registering progress. Of course, such a dream also gives one a further step.

He pursues the forward edge of the dream. Question #9 had the biggest change effect: Get a picture of Riley, now vividly. "When I got an image of him I lunged at him!! Whew... A lot of anger coming loose. Hmm. Let it flow through! Fuckin' right, I'm letting it. [Kicks the wall several times; plaster falls.] It feels good for that to come loose."

Now I shouldn't stop too quickly. Stay with it a while.

RECURRING THEMES SHOW PROGRESS

If you write your dreams down and look back over them, you will notice certain themes again and again. Then you can see your change (or lack of it) in how the stories present that theme. For example:

> 1. The Nazis had taken over. We could be shot any time, and it was certain that we would be, sooner or later. I went through some room and wasn't shot yet, but it was no use fighting back or hiding.

> 2. It was a Latin American dictatorship. Lynne and I were in a hotel. I said, "Let's get out of here, let's take a train today." I expected she wouldn't want to go and I'd give in and stay, but she said O.K. So we packed.

> 3. The Russian Communists had control. I could be shot any time. Then a man came in with a gun and aimed it at me, there was a moment of terror. Then he put the gun down and called me by my name. He'd recognized me, and he was another person just like me!

In the third dream there is something new: Someone armed is on his side. It's touch and go for a moment, but the gun is now turned against his enemies. The man is on his side. Conclusions would be speculative, but there is a sign of progress in the story, here.

For other examples, see Chapter 18.

GREATER DIRECTNESS SHOWS PROGRESS

According to Bonime (1962), progress in therapy can also be seen in dreams this way: At the beginning of therapy, the feelings in dreams may be highly symbolized (explosions and fires for anger; shit for fear; etc.) Later in therapy these feelings are actually felt in the dream, in situations that make them plain.

A research measure (Hendricks and Cartwright, 1978) has been developed for measuring change in dreams.

Bonime also finds a change from inanimate things through insects and bugs to higher animals, such as bears, lions, cats, and humans.

When the woman who dreamed of the dolphin in the dark water was told that large, healthy animals might stand for good life forces, the relief made her cry. In the crying she could feel *that* stirring in her.

Such dreams show progress, as well as pointing to a further step the person has not yet taken. (Her frightened first reaction shows she had not yet taken it.)

When such changes occur in your dreams, they corroborate the progress you know you're making. Of course, you need to check that directly.

As you see from many of my examples, the dreamer is often the last person to interpret a dream as positive and as showing progress. So be careful not to fall for the tendency you probably have—to see no progress in yourself. But if there really doesn't seem to be any, tackle some new action steps. Sense what you are avoiding in yourself, then go very easily and gently with that. Just don't forget it for very long.

Chapter 18

Grounding Dreams

Many people have recurrent dreams about the ground level. They dream they are off the ground and are having trouble getting down to it. They may be perched precariously on a cliff. Or an elevator goes up but not down. Stairs are rickety. Airplanes have landing difficulites, and so on.

Question #11 already alerted you to this theme.

In our society even tiny infants are made to sleep separately from their mothers. There is a dearth of good, solid body contact. That may be why so many people have such dreams and trouble with the ground.

Because the theme is so common, we devote a chapter to it.

What is "being well grounded"? It is a bodily way of feeling and living, not just an idea. To have *only the concept* of ground is to be ungrounded, of course. The following descriptions are meant to evoke a bodily way of feeling the ground.

Being on the ground does not mean losing your heights. Consider the common phrase: "having your feet on the ground." It is about your feet. Your head may be quite high. *Low and high are not contradictory; they make each other possible.* To change metaphors: The roots enable a tree to reach up and spread out high in the sky.

When you lie on your back in the grass, you can feel the whole earth under you. The earth doesn't have to strain to support you. Your support is not precarious. The ground holds you with ease, solidly, as an adult can hold a child. You can exhale all the way, stop being careful, let go, just be. A solid hug can also be like that.

When compared with the infinite sky, the earth seems finite, solid, right here. But infinity can be found in all directions, if one goes far enough. In its own way the earth is also infinity: It takes anything and remains the same. Infinity plus anything is just again infinity. Lightning could kill you, but the earth absorbs it easily and remains the same.

The Jewish mourning ritual involves sitting on the ground. The ground can stand the sorrow which nothing can assuage.

The ground gives strength. We push off from it or brace against it to move something heavy. The strongest people can move nothing when they are hanging from a rope, suspended off the ground.

In contrast: What bodily way of feeling and living is without the ground? We stand on some precarious contraption, like a rickety ladder. Life is precarious. We are shaky, constantly nervous. Thin ice. Watch your step. Be careful. Stay tense. Stay mobilized.

One comedian says he doesn't trust airplanes. He looks as if he is sitting, but he says he never lets his weight down.

In that mode a person's capacities are not all available. Many thoughts, feelings, and ways of action which would occur to the whole organism do not come. The organism is divided when some of it must strain to hold up the rest. A securely grounded organism can do a lot more than a floating, self-holding one.

So it is progress when dreams indicate change from precariously perched to grounded.

Here is one such sequence. These are one person's four dreams over a year's time.

GROUNDING SEQUENCE

First Dream: New Soul
I am riding my bike. I am kind of unsteady on it. I am bringing my shoes to the shoemaker. The shoemaker looks at them, and they have big holes on the bottom. "We'll give you a new sole," he tells me.

I asked him Questions #1 and #2. I saw a double meaning in the word "soul," but he didn't mention that. He described feeling "shaky" on the bike in the dream.

I asked: Can you sense this "shaky" now, in your body?

"..... yes, a little, not very much."

I asked Question #3: What in your life feels shaky, like that?

"Nothing. Things seem very secure these days."

I was eager to ask Question #13: What does "soul" mean to you?

"Well," he said, "the sole is the part of the shoe that stands on the ground."

I was disappointed that he didn't see the pun the way I did, but of course I went on from what he said. I tried filling that into the dream-story:

Does the part of you that stands on the ground need something?

He was already moving that way. "I don't have my feet on the ground too well. I could say that. I'm very idealistic, everybody always says that to me. But I am not about to drop my best values, either, I don't care what they say."

Oh, of course you wouldn't want to do that. But apart from your ideals, why do you say you don't have your feet on the ground too well?

"I'm not too practical, generally. My wife is better at it."

Can you get a body-feeling of this 'not practical'?

"Hmm," he said. "Sure. It feels like being 'shaky' on my bike!"

Stay with that a little.

"I've never been sure of myself. If I let myself feel how I was on the bike, that's what it's like. I know that's what it is!"

I asked more questions, but we didn't get further. I realized we had passed by what came with bodily certainty. So after a while I asked him, What was the most important thing we got to, so far? He said it was this shaky feeling, which he always has, underneath.

I asked him to be a shoe's sole standing on the ground. But he didn't want to do it.

I did try out my own idea. I said, Well, a "soul" is also like the human soul. The dream said, "We'll give you a new soul." But he didn't make anything of that.

Second Dream: Rope

I am hanging at the bottom of a rope. I am holding on. It is too far to the ground, so I can't jump. I don't know how long I can hang on. I woke up scared.

He said, "There must be pretty bad stuff down there, if I'm so scared to drop down."

Like most people, he gave his dream the worst interpretation.

I asked him, Do you have a sense of that, what you call "bad stuff"? I mean, is it like some flavor, some feel in your body? Or are you just thinking that?

"I don't know. No. I was just figuring it must be so if I'm scared."

Do you feel that scared, just now?

"Only vaguely," he said.

Can you let a little of that come in your body now?

He shook his head.

The questions didn't do much. We asked them and let them go. Loving dreams is more important than straining to something.

Third Dream: Valley

I am a doctor. I am on top of a mountain. In the valley there has been an accident. Someone is hurt. I try to go directly down on the steep side of the mountain. I get part way down, too far to pull back up, but I can't let go. I will die if I let go. Then I pull myself up, with all my strength, and I go and take the car. I drive down just fine and cure the hurt people.

He thought he knew what it meant: "I think I have to stop trying to be up so high, with such big ideals and ambitions."

Are you sensing some relief, does it feel right in your body as you say that?

"No. It doesn't feel good to give up on myself."

I see. You are pushing that message on yourself.

"Yes, right."

In the dream, how did you feel when you went down and cured the people? (Question #2)

"Oh, great. I felt like I was really doing it, like a hero."

Can you get that body-feel, just now, a little?

".... Hmm .... That feels good. But a person can't expect to be a hero, can they?"

His sour view of himself had interrupted us. I asked him to have again the felt sense of going down into the valley.

He did again, and seemed to feel very good.

I urged him: Just let it be there for a little while.

He got impatient and wanted to go on. I thought this was a pretty good result already.

I asked Question #10: Suppose whoever is hurt, down in the valley, is a part of you. Can you sense that part, way down?

"No," he said immediately.

Well, if you come down into your body to feel it—what might that be?

He sighed and was quiet for a long time. Then he said, "Oh, sure, I know what that is. A lot of it is from long ago. I avoid feeling it, but I know. You said I didn't have to tell you."

Of course not. I'm glad you got it for yourself. You might want to stay with it a little, just now.

He sighed and did, a little. Then he said, "Let's go on."

I asked Question #6: I said, So the dream story might be that you go down into the valley to cure this part of you.

"Curing myself?"

Well I don't know. That's just what comes to me. What do *you* get if you fill this hurt part into the dream? You go down and cure it, right?

"I would love to," he said. "It doesn't seem so heroic to cure yourself. But it would be good, if I could."

Can you feel being the doctor again?

He didn't look like he wanted to, but he tried for me. He couldn't.

I asked Question #14: Suppose the mountain is an analogy for being up in your head, and the valley is attending down in your body. Does saying that do anything?

He sighed again, and was quiet. Then he laughed. "Yes, that's right. I'm scared to go down there! I could be a hero and let myself down in there anyway, into my body. But I'm scared I'll get to a bad place, like I did in the dream on the side of the mountain. It all fits now!"

You were able, just now, to go down there to the hurt place, and it gave you the hero feeling?

"Yes! But I'm not sure I could do it again alone. I think it's easier when you're asking me questions. I think you must be the car in the dream, that lets me come down the easy way."

Everybody finds it easier with company, I said. But I didn't think I was his car. The dream could have had me in it, but it didn't. It had this car. But I didn't argue. I just asked Question #13. What would you say, if I asked you: What is a car? What is a car for?

"Something you drive."

Could you get a body sense of this?

He sighed. "Back down into my body? Well, let's see. ..... Sure, it's a sense of being solid, in control. I steer it. That's a good way to feel. I actually liked coming down into my body this time, because that's how it feels. That's great! It's just what I need, not to be scared. I want to stop with that one."

There were other dreams between these, including at least one in which something very threatening turned out to be all right. He made various changes in his life, partly from working with dreams. Among other changes he left more time for what he called lying on the beach (which included everything but work). One day he called to tell me a dream. His pleasure in telling it showed that it needed no work to interpret it.

Fourth Dream: Kite
I am lying on the beach, on my back, and I am flying a kite. I am holding the string in my hand, and the kite is far up in the air.

Congratulations, that's great! was all I said.

The series indicates progress, as discussed in the last chapter. Getting to the ground seems very scary and impossible in the second dream. In the third it is impossible at first, then possible in another way (with the car). In the fourth he is supported by the ground and holding a string that is continuous all the way up to the kite.

He had been so sure that "down" must mean less high aspirations. But the kite has both the ground and the sky. Being on the ground does not mean giving up the heights! It makes us continuous rather than precarious.

These dreams taught me again neither to push people beyond what feels right to them nor to take one dream as absolute. The rope dream seemed to say there is no way. But soon the mountain dream said there is a way.

When you have heard many dreams about grounding, you recognize them easily. Here is a similar sequence. By now you can imagine the person's work with them. So I omit it. Here are just the dreams.

ANOTHER GROUNDING SEQUENCE

Like science fiction, there was a problem on earth, very urgent. I and some others went up in a space ship to find the Superior Being, the Life Force, to get help. We came to it, but didn't know how to communicate to it. So I just told it the problem. Some fighter escort planes came up to welcome us from down there. I was scared the Life Force would take that as aggressive, that it would leave, so I told the planes to go away and they did. The Life Force went to work and solved the problem. There were white lights where the problem was, in three places, on the ground. One was in some skyscraper.

[Same night] I was in the bathtub, and my little girl [he doesn't have one] jumped out the window. It was high up in a tall building. Near the ground she flapped some kind of cardboard wings and landed safely. I went down and told her not to do that again. She said it was safe and that she had solved a problem for a whole

rash of kids that had jumped out windows recently. I sent her to bed. (I think I took her clothes off so she wouldn't go out.)

[About a year later] I was walking along the expressway which was built up, as it often is, on an embankment. I was on my way home. Since I was walking, I thought I didn't need to go all the way to the exit, and then come back as I do when I drive. When I got near the closest spot to my house, I saw a good spot to get down. It was a kind of dune there. But suddenly I slid down much too fast and injured myself. I was taken to the hospital. Then I recovered, but I spoke oddly. I thought I might be pretending to be still ill or brain-damaged.

[Several months later] I was in a fast-moving river. I couldn't control how fast I was going. You were behind me, somewhere.

[A week later] I was driving down a sandy hill. The car started going too fast. I was able to stick my foot out and brake the car with my foot.

[Three weeks later] I was a kid and I was sliding down a banister in an old apartment house hallway. The banister turned almost right-angle corners, but I found that by ducking down and shifting my weight I could get around them all right. I was going a little too fast, but it was O.K. You were walking down the stairs ahead of me. We got all the way down to the ground.

Compare the two sequences. Despite the unique imagery of each person, can you see the similarity?

Again, here an early dream says going down is dangerous. It is good that our method does not involve pushing a person in any way. Neither do we assume that any dream gives the final word. The dreamer did a lot of living and changing over this period.

Here is another example:

Peruvian Peasant Dream

A man was crouching on the ground. He was a Peruvian peasant. There were some people up above him somewhere who would hurt him.

What are your associations?

"Well, we live in North America, and then there is Central America which is a very thin connection. And then, way under that, is South America, and it's very big again.

"Peru is on the back side of it. It's the small of its back, sort of.

"Now I'm being that peasant. I'm being tortured or something like that."

How might the dream continue?

..... Nothing happens.

What might that Peruvian do next?

..... "Oh, he got up! And the whole way my stomach was, changed! I can feel sort of, the ground under my feet to push off from. Uh, it feels so simple, very strong and simple. It's, umm, way down there. I almost don't feel it. But it's there."

This example well describes how the ground is sometimes sensed as "way down there," deeper than a feeling.

Focusing and body attention help to move toward grounding. But the felt sense is not itself the ground. A felt sense can be gotten deliberately, almost any time. The ground may come slowly of its own accord, after a while. Then it can be sensed. Our relation to it changes gradually, from underneath.

Chapter 19

A Dream Can Give a Sounding

Earlier I spoke against letting a dream make a decision between two alternatives in a situation. I don't think the dream can do that alone. I emphasized that steps come in a conversation between you and your body.

If you are willing to keep some skepticism with you, we are now ready to see in what way a dream can say something on its own.

In the last two chapters we saw that a series of dreams on one theme can show growth. Each dream gives what I call "a sounding" of how that theme stands, just then. That is easy to see when there is a sequence. But a single dream can sometimes give a sounding too.

Here is an example: After many years of working with dreams, and with himself, one man still found himself sexually blocked due to some awful early experiences. He was also otherwise still stopped and dissatisfied. Recently he dreamed:

Prehistoric Animal Dream
I was standing on a path in the woods with someone. Then a prehistoric animal came out of the bush and onto the path. At first I thought it seemed menacing, but then, very soon, it didn't. When we turned to go on ahead, the prehistoric animal came behind us. It was following us at our own rate.

I felt quite free to congratulate the man on this dream. Can you see why? The prehistoric animal, the basic animal life in him, has (at last) come out of the bush. It is now "on the path"! It is coming behind him, not chasing or threatening, but going at the same rate as he.

Until now I urged you to try to get a step from a dream. I made that clear enough. But at times one can be quite satisfied just with the sounding the dream offers. Knowing this man, I was inwardly moved by his dream. He was even more moved by it and what it announced. That is quite a lot for one dream.

I have no rules to offer for how much to do, or just which questions to ask, except the dreamer's individual feeling. There isn't anything one should *always* do. In this instance neither he nor I felt it appropriate to ask Question #8, and "be" this animal.

Sometimes a dream speaks clearly enough, yet we are glad to have "corroboration" from a second dream. When two of them speak quite clearly, we feel sure.

The same man a week later dreamed:

Nuclear Physics Dream
I was working with nuclear physics and rockets. In the dream I was surprised that I knew how to handle these things. I thought "Gee, I didn't realize I knew this stuff."

Nuclear physics and rockets make us think of dagerous things, explosions, anger, perhaps, something like that. Here his conscious, usual knowledge of himself is that he can't handle that stuff, but the dream says he can. He is surprised.

But, one *can* always force some other interpretation. How can we know when to take a dream as a sounding and when to insist that contradictory interpretations can be resolved only by a growth step? We don't know it for certain and should not bank crucial actions on it.

Another question: Why not try to reverse these "sounding" interpretations with BIAS CONTROL? We do not do it because these interpretations are already in a new direction. The BIAS CONTROL is aimed chiefly at one's usual attitudes and especially at one's superego interpretations. Let us see if we can recognize the difference clearly.

In the above examples the reverse interpretations would express the man's usual attitudes. He would view the animal as dangerous, and he knows nothing of nuclear physics. These two dreams already reverse his usual attitude so that he is surprised in the dream. At first he thought the animal menacing, but then it was not. In the other dream he thought, "I didn't realize I knew this stuff."

So, if the dream puts you into a place that is new for you, you need not reverse that. You would get back to your old usual attitudes.

You know whether your attitude is usually very positive toward yourself or whether you are usually down on yourself. The typical superego attitude is negative and sour. It is not hard to know what would be the reverse of one's usual attitude.

Another help is found in the dream's own detail. In using BIAS CON-
TROL one can often notice how drastically one's first view ignored or
changed certain aspects of the dream.

Example: Dead Duck Dream

Just before I woke up I seemed to hit the ground, head first. And
there was a yellow duck there. The sun was shining and the ground
was a very bright tan. The duck was in the light and very yellow.

The dreamer reports: "I thought immediately: I know what this
means. I'm a dead duck. Certainly. It's a perfect picture of that expression. I felt bad. I was sure it was announcing my death. I read a novel
that ended with a soldier getting killed, hitting the ground like that.

"But then I said to myself: 'I'm always afraid of dying, getting a
terrible illness, and so on. That wouldn't be new. Work for a step from
it, that feels like more life.'

"Then I realized the sun was shining. The duck reminded me of a
mother bird I once saw on the ground, sitting on some eggs in a little
hollow. The whole scene was very lovely and bright. The duck in the
dream was alive. It was not dead. 'Dead duck' was a stupid interpretation. But at first it seemed 'the only' way to read it."

So it helps to look back at the dream and notice the details you may
have violated in a first interpretation. These, together with his typical
negative attitudes, help us know not to reverse his second interpretation.

Sometimes a dream explicitly states a message. Depending on who
says it, and how, it may be accepted.

For example, one woman found herself in a confused and upset
period. Listening to her I was fairly sure it was that "good" kind of con-
fusion: more inner change happening than one can understand. But I was
not sure, and she was even more unsure. "I can't understand what's going
on," she kept saying. "I keep trying to figure it out." Then she dreamed:

Animals in the Water Dream

In a large pool there were some very big animals. They were
rhinoceroses I think. They took my glasses and broke them. They
gave me just one eye glass, and they said if I didn't behave, they
would break that one too. I was so mad!! The man whose pool
it was said, "Those animals have been here for a long time and
they never hurt anybody."

"'I love all animals,'" she said. "But I have never liked the rhino.
I don't know why. I just don't like it."

Here again the dream speaks clearly. Animals are generally good life forces, in accord with instinct and nature. In animals the aggressive and gentle feelings are integrated and appropriate. These particular animals are important; they could not be larger! They break what she uses to see with—as if they spoke directly to her insistence on "figuring it out." And on top of all that, the owner of the pool who would know these animals best, and is in charge of the whole scene, says they never hurt anyone. It is also significant that they have been there for a long time—in her, we would say. I would trust a dream like that.

Another example: Barbara was sure, last year, that she had worked through what happened to her with her (dead) father. Now she dreams:

Father Not Dead Dream
I invited a lot of people to my father's funeral. But A and R and S came, one after the other, and told me: "Your father is still alive." Then N came, and very gently and slowly, as if with compassion for me, said: "This will be hard for you. He isn't dead, Barbara."

Barbara had thought she was done with what happened to her with her father. Would she go far wrong if she tentatively assumed that the dream shows she isn't?

Getting a step does not preclude getting another from the same dream. In that respect a step need not be the interpretation.

I have been telling one young man (as I tell everyone) that the child part of us is very important and needs space and attention, kindliness, and lots of room. Don't wall off your child. Creativity, spirituality, sexuality, and love of life involve our inward child. Sometimes he and I tell each other our dreams. In a recent one he was taking care of a little child. Suddenly the child disappeared. He went frantically looking for it, but it was gone. He was very scared and sad. The dream led him to sense what had happened the previous day, and he reversed a decision which he had made from a bitter, non-playful feeling.

Today he told this dream:

The Child Understands Dream
In the dream I woke up from a dream. I couldn't figure the dream out. But I had a child, and my child could understand it. So I called you up and I said, "I can't interpret this dream but my child understands it." You said, "Hooray," and you were glad.

I said "Hooray," and I was glad. It tells me that this direction I have been selling is probably right for him. It also says that his child-part understands what is currently coming inside him, of which I know little. This is all I need to know.

I have now described how and when it seems to me that the dream gives a "sounding" of where things are and seems to speak clearly.

Am I now urging you to be superstitious about dreams after all, despite everything I said earlier? Am I now saying that one can interpret a dream even without a little step that feels like growth? No, I am just presenting both sides of this issue. We don't ultimately know. And we cannot decide issues like that. The very fact that we would have to "decide" shows we don't know.

Chapter 20

Instructions for
Not Following Instructions

Isn't it wrong to publish instructions for interpreting dreams, and for inward personal process?

One danger with a set of instructions is that people might use them to close off other ways. Anything human involves more than one method to get at it. One person's understanding cannot be enough. Please notice, I don't say this method is all you need or might find valuable. Had I said that, I hope you would have thought me stupid.

Anything you learned here can go well with anything else that you may find helpful. If there seems to be a contradiction, go easy. Let your own steps find the way to reconcile the contradiction.

There are other reasons one might not like specifics, such as are in this book. Instructions may seem to diminish the mystery and openness of dreams—although that is not intended.

Also, written instructions cannot avoid misunderstandings. No formula fits every person. Anyway, one must find one's own path.

These problems occur not only with dreams, but with all types of knowledge about humans.

Adopt a "split-level" approach to all instructions: On the one hand follow the instructions exactly, so that you can discover the experiences to which they point. On the other hand be sensitive to yourself and your own body. Assume that only sound expansive experiences are worth having. *The moment doing it feels wrong in your body, stop following the instruction, and back up slightly. Stay there with your attention until you can sense exactly what is going wrong.*

These are very exact instructions for how not to follow instructions!

And, of course, they apply to themselves, as well.

In this way you will find your own body's steps, either through the instructions, or through what is wrong with them.

Notice: As usual I am asking you to focus, in this case on whatever does not feel right. Focusing is always like that: You don't push on if it doesn't feel right, *but you don't run away either*. You go no further, but you back up only a little, so that *you stay until what is in the way becomes clear*.

Interpeting dreams is quite safe, and so is focusing. They may not work but they are not negative. So, if you sense something that does not feel life-forward and sound in your body, sense what that is until that opens.

But isn't it the height of self-contradiction to give exact steps for how not to follow instructions? Indeed, and so is life, very contradictory. One often needs several attitudes at once.

In a society increasingly skilled at human processes, of course we share the specifics we learn. Shall we teach the specifics of driving a car and not the specifics of interpreting dreams? But, on the other hand, human processes give rise to more different specifics than can be logically consistent. Human nature is not fixed and not knowable in some single system. That is fortunate. No knowledge can push you out of the driver's seat of your life. Especially not our knowledge here, which purports to be about how to find *your own process!*

Therefore this knowledge, here, must arrange for itself to be superseded by you, as you sense for what feels sound, inside you.

Instructions for not following instructions are the essence of focusing—one's own inwardly opening steps.

If you stop and sense what's wrong at any point, and if you wait there until that opens and reveals itself, you can make good use of all sorts of methods and instructions. You do any method better than its author can arrange.

Appendix A

Theory of the Living Body and Dreams

Theory of the Living Body and Dreams

How can the body tell stories and how can it provide complex life-steps that have never existed before? What we have described and experienced does not fit the usual concept of the body. We must think about the living body in a different way. Then we will discuss the nature of dreams.

If you don't like this theory, don't let it get in the way of the experiential steps the book describes. They are not based on theory. You don't need the theory for them. That is why it is an appendix, here.

Theory does *not* ground what I described in the book. I love theory, but it does not ground life. Many people think everything is "based on" theory. If that were so, what would theory be based on?

But can I be sure that my theory did not determine the experiences I described? Granted, theory affects what we experience. A welter of theories is implicit. But further experiencing changes the implicit theories; it is *not* just determined by them. Conceptual forms are not the only order of experience and do not explain all its changes.

I. THE LIVING BODY

1. A NON-LOGICAL THEORY OF THE STEPS

Steps of the sort I described cannot be explained by the usual, logically consistent scheme. The steps change such forms and schemes. They are *non-logical steps*. We must therefore let such steps into our theory, and let them change what theory is.

Before I discuss a new conception of the body, let me ask:

2. HOW DID PEOPLE ARRIVE AT THE USUAL CONCEPT OF THE BODY AS MERELY PHYSICAL, VIEWED APART FROM BEHAVIOR?

All humans seem to have the same body, yet they behave differently. So it seems that the body is one thing and behavior another.

In different cultures life patterns vary. People have different family patterns and different kinds of houses. They eat different things, make love under different conditions, and raise their young differently. If you look for what all humans have in common, you find very little. Yet they have roughly the same "animal" body. So the body has been thought of as universal but *without its own innate behavior patterns*.

If you drop out what is culturally various, you have left what I call *"the remnant body."* It seems to be without life-patterns of its own. Culture and society seem to add the patterns.

Freud thought that the individual body lacks life-patterns. He said that only society teaches these. What he called the "ego" has to learn these patterns. Without them, the body would have hunger and sexual desire but no way to act on them. A desire without any particular pattern is called a "drive." He said that the body ("the it") is a "cauldron of chaotic drives."

That is how Freud thought of biology—as a chemical source of energy *without behavioral patterns*.

When body and biology are viewed in this way, animal bodies also seem to be mere chemistry. Therefore Freud and most scientists of his time thought that the animals must *learn* their complex living patterns.

The study of animals during the past fifty years has revolutionized all that.

3. THE BODY IMPLIES BEHAVIOR PATTERNS

It has been discovered that every animal has complex behavior patterns that are inborn, not learned.

Spiders do not learn to spin their intricate webs; they inherit this behavior pattern. Squirrels know to bury nuts without ever learning it. If you give a nut to an adult squirrel that was raised from birth alone in a cage and is out for the first time, it will bury the nut. A male rat who has never seen other rats will build a nest if its brain is stimulated in a certain way.

At first the scientists tried to find some learning to explain these behaviors. Some researchers even investigated whether these behaviors might be learned in the womb while the mother performs them. Sufficient experiments have now excluded every possibility of learning. Very complex inherited behavior patterns have been found in all animal species.

No human or animal body is mere drives. The body includes be-havior patterns. The "remnant body" of mere drives is only a fiction.

No one now disputes that.

The body includes very complex patterns of interaction between the animals, and with what is around them.

The actions your body desires were not given by culture. Culture only elaborated already complex animal patterns.

But how can a physical "thing" like a body have patterns of behavior and interaction in it? And how do the patterns come to change and vary?

4. HOW CAN WE THINK OF A BODY WITH LIFE-PATTERNS?

In current biology, the concepts of cells and tissues do not let us think about how behavior could be in a body. New scientific concepts are only just beginning to be fashioned for that inquiry.

But it is not mysterious. You inherit not only your chest and lungs, but also the way they breathe.

The way a structure works lies in how it is built. We inherit our internal organs *and* the way they work. The glands, heart, and stomach are not just physical structures; their intricate *actions* are inherited too.

These actions are not only inside the body. The stomach is so struc-tured that it digests certain things that live on the outside. All parts of the body are in interaction with other animals and with the earth and the plants.

The cat's body-sense *implies* how mice run and where they hide. A cat loves holes and cannot pass them up. Its soft paws silence its coming. Its body senses how it will stalk a hole, chase a mouse, or fight with another cat. Each animal's body *implies its interaction* with other ani-mals, and with the trees, the ground, or the water.

If you are a land animal, the ground you walk on is part of how your feet are built, and not only your feet. The muscles up into your thighs, your posture, and the whole balance of all your organs already include the ground against which you press when you walk. The sensation and internal feel-quality of all your organs and muscles comprehend how you walk on solid earth. Your walking-pattern is *implied* in the feel of your whole body.

You can physically feel the space behind you. If there is someone following you on the street at night, your body-sense includes what might happen and the possible ways you might act.

So the body senses its possible behaviors and the circumstances and people with which they might occur.

5. STORIES

The human organism makes up stories two hours out of every twenty-four! Stories are obviously a very basic aspect of humans. What are stories? Situations in which characters interact. The sleeping body, lying there all by itself, implies and senses complex sequences of interaction in situations.

The higher animals all dream; we know it from their eyeball movements during sleep. Culture is not just added to animal patterns. But it does elaborate and change the patterns. Human patterns now exist only in their cultural elaborations.

Human bodies sense complex steps of action and speech.

6. THE BODY KNOWS THE LANGUAGE

When you open your mouth to speak, the words come. From where? From the body. When they don't come, there is little you can do about it. People like to say the words are stored in the brain. But more than the brain is involved. When a familiar word doesn't come, there is a unique bodily sense of that word. In an odd situation, when you find no way to use words, *you feel the new word-use you cannot devise*. The body knows the language. The only way to get right words is to let them come.

Language includes situations as well as words. It is not "just verbal." It brings with it the bodily feel of living in the situations. Words change situations. Human situations are lived and changed largely by talking.

In an odd situation new phrases and actions come out.

How do new patterns arise?

7. HOW ARE NEW BEHAVIOR PATTERNS POSSIBLE?

A new pattern can occur although the animal never did it before. For example, an animal that lives on solid ground instantly produces a new and different walk on sand. Dropped into water, it tries to "walk" but thrashes instead. Its motions are new; they are more and bigger than walking. *A new sequence can occur without having been in the body's repertory.* It happens when a standard sequence *would* have come, but the environment in which it occurs has changed.

The behavior also comes out different if the body has changed. An injured leg makes for a complicated limp that was not in one's repertory. In depression some muscles stay tense, other muscles must work in a new way. One's walk is new.

If the body's behavior came only in fixed repertory units, then, when these cannot be performed, nothing at all would be done. Instead, a new pattern happens; the body's behavioral reportory is not limited.

Even a simpler animal, say an ant or a bug, does not do nothing if it can't do as usual. A new pattern occurs in new circumstances. The ant crawls in a more elaborate way on a fuzzy rug. Its body implies its usual crawl, but on the rug it comes out as never before.

What happens need not consist of pieces that happened before. The new pattern is how the old one comes out when there was some change. Behavior comes from the body-and-its-environment. Change in either brings about changes in the other, which makes for further changes in both.

So a more intricate new pattern can come out of the body.

8. IN A BODY-SENSE MUCH IS INTERRELATED

When the stranger is following you, your body-sense implies what that person might do, and many courses of action you might take. It includes the buildings that block or might help your escape, the other people on the street or their absence, your strength and whatever objects you might use to defend yourself. These things are interrelated in your body-sense. You can think of only a few of them. But a great many possible moves and their effects are implicit and interrelated. How you sense (and would do) one move is implicitly honed by other possible moves. Each is in the space that includes the others.

When at last you do move, it is in interaction with these many things. You move in the sensed space of these inter-affecting possibilities.

It would be logical to say that this sensed space interrelates "all" the possibilities. But later we find some that were ommitted. More importantly: There is no "all." One possible move might turn into many more, in various ways. These are not separate to begin with.

In the logical notion of "interrelating," each piece is the same whether it is in or out of relation to other pieces. That is not so, here. If we were to use a logical scheme, we would not understand the bodily interrelating. The body is much more than and different from what it has been thought to be. Our bodies have already used and changed the words "body" and "interrelating" in interrelation with being followed at night. Our theory is about that interrelating.

9. HOW CAN THE BODY SENSE A STEP THAT CANNOT HAPPEN?

When the old ways don't work, a new behavior may come, as we said above, simply because the old behavior comes out differently. *In that case you do not first have a sense of a new way.* You begin to run in an old way which comes out new, because body and environment are different.

Typically, in such situations, we feel only the usual ways plus why they won't do. They don't "add up" to a new way. We are stuck. But at rare times the body can "add them up" in a single wholistic sense of a new step, even though the step cannot form an action. That is a felt sense.

That unfamiliar, indefinable, single sense is a next step, but only as a bodily sense, not in words or actions.

Such a sense is not disordered or indeterminate. It includes the possible actions and why they won't do, but it is also a jelled, single sense of what needs to happen. This sensing has *more order* than the old patterns.

10. MORE THAN FINISHED EVENTS

Ordinary experience consists of the usual feelings, words, actions, and happenings. I call these familiar things "finished events." Each familiar thing is already an interrelation of all that it involves.

If a felt sense comes, it is a new interrelating. The felt sense is more ordered than the finished events. I call it *"more than finished."*

11. EXAMPLES OF SENSED STEPS
THAT HAVE NOT YET FORMED

In many contexts we find people sensing more intricate steps than as yet exist as patterns. After "that" is sensed for a while, new actions or words may form as well.

You have sometimes sensed a step that could not yet be done. You have been in situations that no known action could meet. You may have felt only the usual actions and why they wouldn't work. Or, you might have got a felt sense of the situation. *That sense is a new step.* It makes finding a doable way more likely, because the sense is an interrelation of more than can usually be interrelated.

In psychotherapy people do not just dig up the past. Nor do they just apply the social patterns they learned. *From the body's felt sense they find more intricate perceptions and distinctions than they ever met on the outside.* The steps of personal healing and development are more intricate than the old patterns of animals or society. But at first they are often just sensed.

The implied new action is not yet formed in such a sense. The action is not all there in the felt sense, yet it can come from that sense. If a way of action comes, then we say it "was" in the felt sense all along. But the word "was" is used in a special way here.

An unfinished poem "needs" an ending. The ending doesn't exist yet. It is not in the lines written so far. Reading the lines over and over, the poet may get a felt sense of the missing ending. The lines very finely *imply* an ending that is not, as such, in the lines.

When an ending does come, the poet must usually revise the earlier lines. The ending was not a logical step from those lines. It shifts their meaning. In the very act of demanding an ending, the earlier lines and patterns also change themselves.

These are familiar examples of sensing a step that has never yet formed. In implying such a step, the old forms change themselves as well.

12. STEPS THAT CHANGE OLD FORMS CANNOT BE DERIVED LOGICALLY

By logic one must begin and end with the same units and patterns. It is not in a logical way that the body implies and interrelates many possible behaviors. A new step does not merely rearrange old pieces. It is often more intricate and very different from whatever happened before.

This kind of step cannot be derived from pre-existing pieces, forms, or ideas. It is not derived logically from the dream, or from the unfinished poem.

Logical steps stay within consistent forms. When the forms themselves change in the act of implying something new, that cannot be derived by a logical step from them.

Logical and non-logical are two kinds of steps.

13. THERE ARE MANY KINDS OF NEXT EVENTS (AND MANY WAYS OF DEFINING KINDS)

The "step" emphasized throughout this book is a very special kind of event. Many other kinds of events could happen next. The organism might die. An old pattern might be repeated over and over. Much else might happen.

Differences between kinds of steps opens a new field of study. We are only just beginning to characterize various kinds of steps, and to differentiate them and their results. The focusing kind of steps can be reliably picked out on tape recordings of psychotherapy. They correlate highly with change and individual development (Mathieu-Coughlan and Klein 1984; Gendlin 1981). These steps have also been found to be related to longevity (Sherman 1984).

Research does not make up facts, neither is it without assumptions. We must still ask: Is the greater order and intricacy of this kind of step an *individual* development? Especially when a step comes "guided" by the symbols from a dream, is it not social conformity in disguise?

14. POLITICAL AND INDIVIDUAL CHANGE

Some universal dream-symbols seem to reflect nature: animals, plants, a body of water, the earth. But they also include cultural political arrangements, wise elders, and heroes who cross the water. Are these political patterns right because some of them are ancient? And of course, current power arrangements are also in our dreams. In the chapter on symbols, I said we should take seriously anything said in a dream by an elder, landlord, desk clerk, conductor, or any person in charge of the premises. Such a person symbolizes someone who knows the place. That makes symbolic sense, but doesn't it also indicate internalized social conformity?

The kind of step we want comes from the interaction between the dream and our responses. The dream alone need not be just "believed."

Dreams lead some people to an abject reverence for ancient patterns, symbols, and rituals. (Jung called them "archetypes.") That is not the recommended attitude. A social pattern (current or ancient) deserves careful but rebellious handling. One cannot just wish it gone. It has energy because it is a life-pattern of the body. But, when its function is lived out differently, its power wanes. And even if we cannot live some of that, the old pattern weakens if our choices and intricate experiences are asserted in a continuing interplay with it.

Many people don't notice that social patterns have elaborated and have become engrained in their bodies. We are more helpless against social patterns when we don't know them as such. Then, when we feel them, we identify with them. We think, "That's just the way I am."

Other people take the opposite view. They deny that anything can originate individually. They say it is an illusion; that we do and feel only what was built into our bodies by society, political power, history, and language. Only these can change the patterns. They say the individual is no source at all.

These views are too simple.

It is true that the self-known person is not the source of the steps we have been discussing. Focusing steps don't come from how you know yourself. They change that. The individual is not some content which explains the steps. A step can change what would be used to explain it.

Nor is "the unconscious" the same before and after the step, so that it could explain the step. What is termed "the unconscious" also changes in such a step. Social patterns are engrained, but they also change in such steps.

No pattern, content, or thing is the being who looks out from each pair of eyes. And only that is important.

Separating individual power and social power oversimplifies them. Society and individual are always both involved, but their relationship is better studied by distinguishing many kinds of steps and processes. For example:

Some patterns are explicitly imposed by social pressure. Others arise freshly from the organism, but in response to circumstances arranged around it, politically beyond its control. Some new patterns develop in intimacy when two people genuinely take each other into account. (If they do not, the engrained pattern probably reasserts its power.) Each kind of step has a variety of responses. Each affects the others. We need to study different kinds of steps.

So far I have tried to show that living bodies sense their complexly patterned behavior possibilities, situations, and stories. In *certain kinds of steps* the patterns change. New, more intricate patterns come. Sometimes these are sensed even though they cannot form.

II. DREAMS

15. WHY DREAMS SEEM TO SPEAK "IN CODE"

Dreams speak metaphorically. Metaphors would be rightly called "code," if ordinary language were different. But ordinary language is itself metaphorical. Words work as metaphors. The word "metaphor" is a metaphor that means "carrying further." It is a metaphorical carrying, not like carrying a package. The word "language" comes from "tongue" *(lingua)* and carries that word further. And "code" comes from "codicils, ancient manuacripts in an ordinary language that we can no longer read.

Metaphorical language is the natural one! Metaphorical carrying further is how words work. Old words come into new uses all the time. A word is not a fixed entity. It is for its further new uses, and it changes in new uses. That is the nature of language. "Nature" (and human nature) are not finished forms. "Nature" comes from *natus,* being born. Nature is metaphorical: it never just is. It *is for* further birth.

A dream does not hide its "message" in metaphorical code. The dream is born metaphorically.

16. THE OLD ACTION-PATTERNS CHANGE WHEN THEY PARTICIPATE IN NEW ONES

A new metaphor carries further how situations are patterned. The old meanings play an essential role, but are themselves "carried further" in that role.

If the word "metaphor" has applied only to words, let it carry further. Then its meaning changes.

Metaphors are not *"just"* verbal. Words change *situations.* A new metaphor changes situations in a new way. Conversely, a new behavior *silently* changes the meanings of implicit words. Then, when these words come from the body, they work differently.

17. ANYTHING MIGHT "CROSS WITH" ANYTHING ELSE

A metaphor brings the word's old situations into a new situation. The two contexts "cross" and form something new.

Any two things can be further "crossed."

For example, how is your anger like a chair? (It just sits? It might get thrown at someone?) If you try it with *your* anger, what comes may be new. How does that work? You let *all about chair* interact with *all about your anger* and—something comes. Then you say it "was" always true of you. But actually it was made by crossing them just now.

"Crossing" is just a simple notion which I use here for a finely relevant organic process. The chair will make *just what can intricately fit* your anger. But that was not, as such, there before. To some extent, the crossing will change and elaborate your anger and what chairs can be.

The change is slight in ordinary experience, since chairs remain chairs and anger remains anger. But there is some novelty.

Crossing seems strange only if you think of each experience as a separate thing lying next to other experiences. Recall my example of someone following you. The move you finally make comes from the sense of all possible moves and results. Any experience is a crossing of many experiences. They *cross* to shape the present one. My word "crossing" changes too. It crosses its old uses with this context, here. "Crossing" says this.

18. SOUND AND VISION

The traditional theory is wrong, that the five senses are originally separate and related only by association. What we "only" see is formed already crossed with what we hear, taste, smell, touch, and with how we live and act in situations.

What we take to be "just" a sound is actually a very complex product. Animals don't hear *sounds*—they always hear other animals, trees falling, complex events. The "mere sound" is a more sophisticated and symbolic human product, not an original element.

Similarly, animals don't see pictures. They see only actual things. To see something and also take it as "only" visual is more complex than ordinary events. Seeing the mere image of the mountain involves seeing the mountain *and* that it is a piece of cardboard. The body's physical implying and crossing is involved when you experience a "mere sound" or a "merely visual" image.

Therefore it can powerfully affect the whole body if you image certain sounds or colors. Many things cross to produce a sound or an image.

The looks of ordinary things remain stable *not* because vision is naturally separated from other experience, but because all the usual relevances have already crossed to produce the ordinary things.

19. PAST EXPERIENCES ARE CROSSED
IN ANY PRESENT EXPERIENCE

The past and the present are not two different things in different time-spots. The past is inside the present. Past experiences participate in shaping the present. In that role, they change. But they are also always still here, and can change in some other way in some other present experience.

Despite new elaborations, the body retains the old forms as well. It never has only its present action-patterns. One can see that in many examples. An embryo reaches the adult state by going through old versions of the body. Freud found that "the unconscious" (the body) retains and can repeat infantile behaviors. The past is always still here.

Crossing applies to all experience: waking, dreaming, and felt sense. Any moment always includes many past experiences "crossing" with each other to form relevant perceptions of a present.

Let us now see what is special about dreams.

20. "UNFINISHED EVENTS" SHOW THE CROSSING

So far we have distinguished ordinary *"finished events"* from a felt sense which I called *"more than finished."* There is also a third type: *"unfinished events."*

All experience involves crossing, but in dreams (and some other "altered states") one can *actually see* the "crossing." One can see it because the crossing is *unfinished,* still going on.

Usually we don't see the crossing. In ordinary experience it is always already finished. We experience the result, not what goes into it.

For example, the person I see walking cannot be my father because my father is dead. Besides, he didn't live in this city. He wouldn't be in this place. These facts go into shaping my experience. As a result, I only see a man who resembles my father. I do not first see my father.

Suppose there is a cement wall between us, so that I see only the man's head moving along. I don't first see the impossible apparition of a floating head, and then correct it. I see the man walking behind the wall.

The familiar objects result, when what bears on an event has already gone into it. The usual thing is the "finished" event.

Suppose an event remained "unfinished." Then it could be crossed and shaped some more. We could see and feel the crossing going on.

In altered states the experiences are not the usual finished packages. The crossing is still going on. I may see my father before I see a man who resembles him. I may see a floating head, and then the wall.

Why are some events unfinished? Why was there less than the usual shaping?

21. WHEN AND WHY DO "UNFINISHED" EVENTS COME?

Dreams, meditation, drug states, stimulus deprivation, and hypnosis may all involve a withdrawal from ordinary bodily interaction. When we sleep we are not talking, walking, and living with people and things.

To imagine something while awake, we also withdraw and relax to some extent. We take our eyes off the events around us. We try not to hear what is being said and not to see the things around us. That helps images and odd possibilities to come.

But past a certain crucial point, in deeper relaxation, the sense of one's body can fade away. The body is no longer in interaction with many of the circumstances and their implications. There is less body-sense. But body-sense is how one interprets situations! Therefore, beyond that crucial point one cannot interpret anything in the usual way. Even ordinary words don't mean all they usually do. Under hypnosis, when told to "raise your hand," the person moves one hand only from the wrist. This narrower way of interpreting shows that some usual relevances have not entered in, when we see and hear. The usual things have not finished forming. In deep relaxation and withdrawal the events are unfinished, still being shaped.

22. IN "UNFINISHED" EVENTS A SMALL ADDITION CAN MAKE LARGE AND UNUSUAL DIFFERENCES

When events are unfinished, any little thing can still cross with much else. Therefore a small thing can make big changes. It participates in the crossing that is still going on.

That is why unfinished events are in their own way more eventful and more open to momentary interaction than ordinary experience.

In some altered states a small facet can enter into how subsequent events form. Its effects can show up in everything else. It is amplified by this crossing with other experiences. A dream can let a small remark from yesterday reveal and develop relevances that affect how everything is pictured. An emotional tone that seemed unimportant can be crossed with much else in the dream.

In unfinished events one facet may enter more things than usual.

23. UNFINISHED, FINISHED, AND MORE THAN FINISHED

I have discussed three kinds of events.

With *"unfinished"* things, when the body is stilled, you may see and touch a chair, but some of the chair-relevances have not gone into it. Then it cannot do everything that things in space like chairs can do.

But something different can still be made from it, which could not be made from finished things. Suppose you are angry at the person who gave it to you. As your anger enters into the crossing, the chair looks different. If it had been a finished chair, anger could no longer be relevant to its looks. Your anger is also not all made. More can enter. It is still being made. The facets which together would make anger are still coming, one by one. You may feel one of them separately, as you never did before. The chair may also change its structure to embody it. If you have a need, the chair may walk over and do something for you. Or it may change itself to picture your need. It can, because it still being made. It is not limited to the usual finished things.

When your experience consists only of *"finished"* things, a chair is just that thing in space. Your anger is just anger. The usual relevances have already crossed to produce them. Chair and anger can still further cross, but only within their usual relevances. You might pick up the chair and throw it out. Or, if you happen to need a piece of wood or cloth, your need becomes relevant to the chair. But, however great your need, the chair can respond only as a chair. Nothing at all may be able to happen from your need. You sit in your room and the need remains stuck, in your body.

In contrast to unfinished and finished, a felt sense is *"more than finished."* In one interrelating it includes all the usual relevances and those which cannot usually participate. The new *felt sense* opens and changes the usual things, words and actions.

Both "unfinished" and "more than finished" events incorporate your need. Both of them open the closed usual things and feelings. But they do it in different ways. We will discuss this difference.

First, let us see how your needs enter into dreams, which are events that have not finished crossing.

24. WHY ARE DREAMS RELEVANT TO WHAT YOU NOW NEED?

Why might a dream bring something valuable? Would it not be a mere jumble?

No, crossing is always "relevant." "Relevance" and "crossing" are really the same thing. What can be relevant to (or can "bear on") an event goes into its make-up. What happens is what *can make itself* relevant.

Therefore not just any mood or remark from yesterday crosses with how people and things look and act in your dream. What comes is what can enter and add to the network of "relevant" crossed connections.

We said that the living body implies its behaviors, what happens next. You don't eat when your body is not hungry. You exhale only after inhaling. What forms next is what your body implies, next. When it cannot happen it continues to be implied. Whatever *can* form from that implying happens.

In "unfinished" events more can form. On the other hand, the body is not fully ongoing, so these new events are not usually the full-bodied step. But we can understand that what forms is just what you need, what is unlived or missing.

"Just what you need" can come in two ways. The dream's events may picture the need, lack, or problem in how you live. More rarely, the dream pictures an answer, how you would live a step toward what is unlived or missing.

25. WHOLENESS IS NOT PATTERNS

Don't we have to know what human "wholeness" is when we speak of needs, of something "unlived" or "missing?" Is it a whole of well known cyclic events, like eating, defecating, getting hungry, and eating again? Each animal is perfect in its way, maturing, building its kind of nest, rearing its young, and growing old in its own perfect way. Some people think that human life consists of such eternal samenesses. But human wholeness is more complicated than that. It involves the development of an *individual* person.

Without *this* individual's *bodily* step, only very general statements can be made about wholeness. Major dimensions can be stated: love, sex, work, art. Someone's way of life might miss, repress, or oppress one of these. That is why a sense of wholeness does come with even a little development of a major left-out dimension.

But those big generalities don't supply your specific next step of development. Nor is wholeness just being well-rounded. There is further development on all of these dimensions.

Human "nature" opens out like a "V" further and further at the top. It does not return and close at its top, as a diamond-shape does. Human patterns are moving further and further away from a closed form, shape, or content.

Every little child is whole. That whole child is still in each of us, inside. But what is this wholeness when one considers adult development?

There is a seeming contradiction. Animals, children and primitives are *more* whole than we. On the other hand, humans are now more developed, and the adult is clearly a development from the child. The child starts whole, but adult development is not just loss! So wholeness exists on many levels. It is not some fixed amount. It is not a content. It is all there at the start and continues working in us at every stage.

Wholeness is not patterns, ancient or current.

26. WHOLENESS WITHOUT A FELT SENSE

But wholeness (and how the word "wholeness" works) must define itself for us from its bodily working.

Suppose a new complex design does not satisfy the artist. *Even without a felt sense of what's wrong,* the artist is stuck for the moment. The design doesn't "work." It is not a complete whole. The body senses not only simple straightness, as when a picture hangs crookedly. It also senses the wholeness of a new design which has never been whole as yet. This needed, unlived complex whole is implied *even without a felt sense, just in being stuck.*

Here the phrase "is implied" means just this quality of being stuck (enough to make the artist pause and not put in just any line).

The phrase "is implied" has a different meaning when there is a felt sense. In our example of an unfinished poem, the ending is implied in the poet's felt sense. But even without a felt sense, the poet knows to stop and pause, not to write what does not work.

Even without a felt sense the body rejects the available moves, and forms only relevant events that can cross with its implying. Even when there is as yet no further step, not even a felt sense, the body's implying seems to "know" the new whole, and what is "missing."

27. NOT PATHOLOGY BUT DEVELOPMENT GOVERNS

But why is there the "unlived" and the "missing"— are they indicative of failure and pathology? They may be due to your development as well. If in some respects you find no way to live, it may be because you have developed so far (and well) that the crude usual ways become impossible for you.

People try to distinguish these two reasons. You might wonder, is this trouble due to my twisted childhood and failure to develop, or is it rather because I am very developed? You wonder, because it seems to be both. You have developed too far for the simple, crude ways, and so you come up against what blocks you from better ways.

The two reasons cannot be split apart.

For example, if you don't develop the capacity to nurture others and empathize with their needs, you may not have to come up against your pathological difficulties in valuing your own needs and perceptions. A development can make some pathological aspects relevant, which would not have been a problem otherwise.

Quite apart from pathology, one development requires others. Your developed empathy now requires what you have *not* developed, for example, how to interact, confront, and negotiate with others.

So, when I speak of "just what you need," what is "missing" or "unlived," that does not mean pathology or a low level of development. On the contrary! As you develop, more further development becomes implied and "missing."

Of course our theory does not really determine what can come in dreams and other states. Theoretical explanations do not legislate what can come. Any explanatory patterns are just that, patterns. We have seen that steps change patterns.

But the theory lets us understand why dream patterns come relevantly and reveal the intricacies of our current lives. Some of these patterns are called "symbols of wholeness" (Jung), but it is not a simpler or older wholeness. The patterns of wholeness come with the intricacy of our current need for a step.

Usually they don't supply the step. Instead, the "patterns of wholeness" cross with and are shaped by our troubles.

28. A DREAM OF "JUST WHAT YOU NEED," BUT WITHOUT THE STEP

Let me first give an example of the usual case. The missing unlived wholeness *does come* in the dream, but crossed with the dreamer's problem, rather than as the step.

The following dream clearly indicates the needed step, but it does not show the step itself. An ancient pattern of wholeness, an animal, is pictured where a development in the person's living is needed.

Mother Pig Dream

I was watching a mother pig which was also me. She had a lot of little piglets. They kept sucking on one tit, and it was very, very sore. She tried to get them to go away, but they wouldn't. So she just lay herself down and let them suck. Then she knew she had to get away, to be by herself and rest. She went into a tunnel,

*and the sun was just on the other side. But she found a plastic
bag in the tunnel, and crawled into it, and died.*

Here the sound, whole animal crosses with the dreamer's nurturance
and concomitant inability to protect herself and to say "no" to people.
The dream is not just her behavior. The dream does bring wholeness.
And it is not just the simpler animal wholeness. The supposedly simpler
pattern of animal wholeness now has the intricacy of her current problem.
But where is the new growth-step? It is in the animal, but the step is
not in the dream.

In the dream the mother pig has the dreamer's problem. (Alterna-
tively, it might have been the dreamer's opposite, violent and ugly in
its left-over form.)

We have to ask the dreamer how she would handle the situation if
she were a mother pig. For a minute she senses physically what would
come. Then, in her body, the step comes: She swats them off. "Not too
hard," she says, "not hurting them, but firmly and abruptly. Flick."

That sounds simple, like an animal mother, but it is the jelled
simplicity of a step from her complex adult current body.

The image was brought by the dream. In ordinary focusing you
might ask: What would my body be like, if this problem were solved?
Sometimes a sound energy of this kind comes. You might also get an
image like that, and work with it as from a dream. But we don't know
if you would get the same image. The dream brought this image.

Focusing brought the step.

29. WHEN THE STEP IS IN THE DREAM

Less frequently, but often, the dream does show the step. (For example, see Ch. 17, Book Award Dream, and Ch. 19, Animals in the Water
Dream.)

Sometimes the step is partially there:

The Secret Dream
*Aunt Cecily came and whispered in my ear that she had a secret
for me. It felt wonderful.*

"That's my one good aunt, the one that bought me the only beautiful
dress that I ever got, in all those years."

From the felt sense the dreamer might experience the step which is
still secret, here. What it is might be inferred in many ways, and one

of them might be corroborated by the bodily coming of a step. But whether that comes or not, the step is in the dream.

Here we would keep repeating the actual dream-image (see Ch. 5): Aunt Cecily has a secret for you. For you. Aunt Cecily has your secret. She has brought a secret for you.

"Aunt Cecily has a secret for me! Every time we say it, it makes a sort of a smile come in me."

To let this step come in a bodily way, we need not know what it is. If we do know, the dream image may still be the best way to let the body keep taking the step.

Even when the step is in the dream, focusing is needed to let the whole, fully ongoing body take the step. The body changes through the bodily coming of the step. The full-bodied coming is not usually possible in sleep.

30. THE "INTEGRATION" DILEMMA

In deeply relaxed states we do not fully appreciate what comes. In a dream we rarely know it is a dream. The body-sense that interprets everything has been relaxed. The whole way we are is not fully ongoing, so all of it cannot respond. The same is true of hypnosis and drug states. Therefore professionals provide a so-called "integration session" after every altered state. We need our whole sense of things back again if we are to evaluate what was new and take a whole-bodied step.

But when our usual state is back, we lose the direct experience of what was new. We only remember it.

So there is a dilemma. We cannot "integrate" what is new when we are in the dream and have let go of the usual. Neither can we do it when we feel as usual.

That is the integration dilemma.

31. FOCUSING: NEW SHAPING WHILE BEING ALL THERE

The crucial point, as we slightly relax, is when we are maximally all there, and also open for *more than finished* crossing and shaping. A full-bodied felt sense can come at that point.

In focusing we relax just to that crucial point. Here is how we recognize that point: It is where we sense the body talking back. "Talking back" means: If there is a problem and we try to say we feel fine, *we can sense a response in the body.* A bodily sense "talks back" with a distinct quality that is not all right. That is the felt sense.

It need not be a problem. Also with something pleasant, if we say why we think it is pleasant, the body can "talk back" with more than what we had thought.

If you relax further, past this crucial point, the body melts away or accepts suggestion.

But at that crucial point focusing can go deeper and deeper. There are two different kinds of "depth."

32. TWO DIFFERENT DIMENSIONS CALLED "DEPTH"

The *depth* of body-narrowing sensory- and motor-inhibition is one well-known dimension. The *depth* of focusing is another kind of depth. Staying at the same crucial point along the one dimension, focusing steps can be slight or very deep on the other dimension.

Some people know while dreaming that it is a dream. That is called "lucid dreaming." If you have that ability, I would recommend not controlling the dream as if to close the channel, substituting conscious constructions. Rather, I would recommend interacting with what comes. Do something, then see what happens. In the Sennoi tribe, which practices lucidity, the dreamer asks the figure why it came and what it has to bring. The dream is then allowed to continue, much as in our question #9.

Some masters of meditation are said to retain their whole bodily sensing in "deep" meditation. They can hear a slight noise that most meditators cannot hear. This also shows that there are two different dimensions of "depth." Nothing I say here is meant to exclude other ways, but perhaps these people can also let a fresh, whole-bodied step form in response to what comes in these states.

At the crucial point one can sense the body talking back. A fresh bodily step can come, forming from all you are and know.

Each such step is a bit of integration. That is why, compared to the flamboyant unfinished events, some focusing steps can *seem* small.

33. "INTEGRATION"

Here the word "integration" means a bodily way, not logic. As professionals have integrated that word in practice, its logical form has changed. It does not mean fitting one more piece in among old ones. Some pieces get thrown out; some change; there is no finite set of "all pieces"; there are not really pieces. The step is a bit of living. It is not a taking in of something. It is a change of the whole, made by the whole body.

I do not know that a felt sense is the only integrative way. I do know that it is integrative.

In a felt sense all of what goes into finished events is brought to that point, yet it is also open.

34. THE COMING OF A "FELT SENSE" IS ALREADY A CHANGE

A felt sense differs from the usual data of consciousness: ideas, events, memories, emotions, familiar packages. These have artificial stability and seeming continuity. But they are products. If we try to explain ourselves with these, we get a false explanation. The body's "implying" is vastly more and different. It is not made of the sort of data that consciousness has in front of it as objects.

A felt sense has the problem as a whole. It is just that odd sense of what's wrong. The usual and more are interrelated, integrated, jelled in the formation of *that* one new felt sense.

But is a felt sense the whole implying? Isn't a felt sense also merely a "datum"? Yes, "that indefinable quality in my body" is a kind of datum, a "that." But the coming of a felt sense is new.

The forming and coming of *any* datum is a production, a change. That change is more than the mere datum you get. For example, the bodily change of anger *coming* in you is much more than "the anger." When a usual emotion comes, you change.

The physical coming of any datum is a change. Unfortunately we often repeat only the same changes, over and over. The coming of a felt sense is a new change, beyond the usual flow of changing feelings.

A felt sense usually requires deliberately setting oneself to sense what is not there yet, and waiting to let it jell and come.

The very coming of a felt sense changes the implicit patterns of action and speech. Therefore new modes of action and speech can then form from it.

35. DON'T REDUCE DREAMS AND FOCUSING TO THEORY

These theoretical concepts do not substitute for dreams or the body. Rather, with dreams and the body we may have improved upon a few concepts.

I began this appendix by saying: If you don't like this theory, don't let it get in the way of the experiential steps the book describes. They are not based on theory. You don't need the theory for them.

I end by saying: If you *do* like the theory, please don't reduce dreams to it.

Theory does not represent what "is." Theory makes sense, but sense-making is itself a kind of step which expands what "was." That opens to even more further steps, and these need not stay consistent with the theory.

Appendix B

How To Use Each Question

How To Use Each Question

Here are the questions, explained in detail. The short introductions are from Chapter 2 and are repeated here in full in reduced type.

QUESTION #1: WHAT COMES TO YOU?

What are your associations in relation to the dream?
What comes to mind as you think about the dream?
Or pick a part of the dream. What comes to you in relation to that?

Before we interfere, we want to see what comes on its own. Once we ask other questions, that might not come any more.

There is also another reason. Even in ordinary situations, if you want to ask or tell people something, it is wise first to let *them* say what they want to tell you. Otherwise they are preoccupied with that and cannot take in what you say. When their channel has cleared, they can take your questions down, in. So it is also with yourself. Before you ask your body questions, let it first tell you what it has to say about the dream.

First, take a minute to receive what comes of its own accord.

Then, if you don't get enough, do that with each part of the dream.

Whatever comes to mind is welcome.

I will tell more about how to use associations after Question #3.

QUESTION #2: FEELING?

> What did you feel in the dream?
> Sense the feel-quality of the dream. Let it come back as fully as possible.
> Choose the most puzzling, oddest, most striking, or most beautiful part of the dream. Picture it to yourself and let a felt sense of it come in your body.
> Or pick one part of the dream.
> *Then ask:* What in your life feels like that?
> Or: What does this feel-quality remind you of? When did you ever feel like that?
> Or: What is new for you in that felt sense?

Most people attend only to feelings they recognize, such as anger, sorrow, joy, jealousy, disappointment—feelings with names. If a feeling has no name, people say it's "nothing." We have to explain that one can pay attention to a feeling one cannot name. A dream (and each part) brings an odd sensation, a nameless quality—the *felt sense*. It is the unique feeling-quality of that part of the dream. "Uhm ... sort of um......hmm ..." You grimace and twist your body oddly because there are no words to convey it. But there it is.

The label doesn't matter. It is *this*. Where and when have you felt *this quality* before?

Named feelings like fear, anger, or disappointment may be in the dream. Even so, the whole quality includes more than you can name. What in your life gives you this angry, this *whole* quality?

Working on dreams with the focusing method trains you to work on other problems in this way. And not only problems. Focusing on the sensed "edge" is often valuable. You want it when you need creativity, *new* ideas, a change in a present constellation. Where does novelty come from? How can something new arise to subtly fit the circumstances? It arises from a felt-sense, the body's total sense of all the facts, past and present—always more than one can think of piece by piece.

Most people pay attention only to the outward aspects of anything, including what they dream. For example, if you say, "What does this place in the dream remind you of?" they will concentrate on the layout of the space. But it is *the feel* of this layout which best gives you the association.

To get this felt sense sharply as you picture the scene, pay attention *to the middle of your body*. Sense what feel-quality the dream-image makes there.

What in your life feels like the dream? Scan your life these days: What are your main concerns? Run through your main situations, problems, parts of your life. Your work. Your relationships. Your struggles. Your plans.

As you scan, you have the felt sense of the dream with you. You ask both: What is like the dream-events? and What *feels* like that?

For example, "That weird quality...of that place in the dream, what situation in my life feels like that? ... [focusing ... nothing comes]. O.K., *what problem of mine feels like that?* ... [focusing ... nothing comes]. It feels sort of familiar..... What else is in my life?----. ----. Aha...."

"What in my life feels like that?" is asked in all the rest of the questions. It hovers with you, as you use the other questions.

When you find something in your life that feels like the dream, don't assume too quickly that the dream is only about that. It might be about a larger issue. This part of your life may only be one instance of the issue. When you identify it, also you might see that it concerns this and many other situations as well.

QUESTION #3: YESTERDAY?

> What did you do yesterday? Scan your memory of yesterday.
> Also recall what you were inwardly preoccupied with.
> Something related to the dream may come up.

Think of yesterday, where you went, whom you saw, talked to, etc. Include what you did inwardly: How were you feeling? What preoccupied you yesterday? As you scan yesterday, slowly, something will relate to the dream. Freud said that every dream has "day residues" in it. Perhaps not every dream, but the dream-making often uses something from that day.

Using Associations:

An association or day residue gives a hint. Sometimes it makes the whole dream clear with a big felt shift and flood. More often nothing moves as yet. *But we keep that association "in the pot."* I can relate each new thing to it and to whatever else I have "in the pot."

Is the dream *about* the day residue situation? Not usually. Say I had a dream about Bob, whom I haven't seen in a long time. Then I remember that I mentioned Bob to Marcia. Is the dream about my relationship with Marcia? Not necessarily. The incident is one of the materials the dream-making used. For what point, I don't know yet.

Once she is "in the pot," Marcia enters into my dream-interpreting. She was not in the dream. I would never have thought of her. *But now I recall that odd feeling I have left from yesterday's talk with her.* Why did I tell her about Bob? Oh, I know that..... Now my felt reason for telling her enters into the total feeling I have of the dream. A little later I suddenly grasp another part of the dream. When I then think again of Marcia, something may pop! Ah....

Freud's basic method of associations was to pursue each association singly. You can do that. With focusing we can use associations more powerfully. Let each association give you its feel-quality, the felt sense. But then also relate some of them to each other and to new things as they come in.

The first three questions can be used throughout the rest of the questions.

With all questions more associations can be tried for.

With all questions, focus on the feel of whatever you examine, and wonder what is like that in your life.

Questions #1, #2, and #3 offer three ways to get associations.

If some associations came, you need not go on and on to get more. You need not ask all three questions. You can come back to them later in relation to any part of the dream.

QUESTION #4: PLACE?

> Visualize and sense the lay-out of the main place in your dream.
> What does it remind you of?
> Where have you been in a place like that?
> What place felt like that?

It may be a mix of several places you remember.

Did the place feel dreary, light and open, safe and comfortable, threatening and strange, familiar, very odd, or how? Sense the feel quality of it; probably it has no word. What place have you been in that ever felt like that?

It may help another person to understand what "feel-quality" means if you suggest several words like that. Explain that they need no word for it. What matters is to focus on it, directly.

Go over the lay-out: Was it a long apartment? What was outside the window? Where have you been in a long apartment like that with a yard out the window, having that heavy feeling to it?

Example: 55th and Lake Park Dream
In the dream it looked just like 55th and Lake Park, but not like now—it was many years ago, before they built what's there now.

This would lead you to ask: Why would the dream place these events into a scene from those years? What went on for you then, which matters now?

QUESTION #5: STORY?

First summarize the story-plot of the dream. Then ask yourself: What in your life is like that story?

Summarize the events of the dream in two or three steps: "first... and then... and then...." Make it more general than the dream. This can be done in several ways, if the first way has no effect.

Example: Crossing the River Dream
I had to cross this river, there was no way across, then I saw a bridge further down but when I got there it was only to an island in the river.

The story-summary might be: "First there seems to be no way, then there is one, but only part way. What in your life is like that?"

Or: "First you're discouraged, then it's better but not all O.K. What in your life is like that?"

Or: "First it's one big gap across. Then it turns out there is a place in between."

Story plot summaries let you ask: What is like that for you? Where in your life are you now lacking a way? What are you discouraged about? What seems like one big gap, all or nothing, right now? What might be like that island?

Can you sense the metaphorical power of the story? Have you ever told a story when you could not say something straight out? You say,

"I feel as if I were lost in a forest, and...." You tell a story about the forest which is really to communicate how you feel.

For example, suppose you just met a new person of the opposite sex. You are excited at the possibility of a new relationship but also nervous and tense. You are scared the person won't like you once they get to know you. Suppose you expressed this in a story, what might it be?

You might say, *"I feel as if* I were applying for an important job. I come into the room and stumble over the carpet because I'm so nervous."

Or, you might tell the story this way: "Someone finds a treasure chest dug in the ground. When they open it, expecting gold, a crawly animal comes out. The person screams and runs away."

The story expresses the feeling and the situation. You can make up a story to convey any feeling.

The best ideas for stories come right out of your felt sense. Rather than inventing it deliberately, you lean back and focus on the felt sense. Ideas for a story will pop. That way you get more than only the ideas you already have in mind.

A dream is something like that, but more participates in making the story than when you are awake.

Even in ordinary talk we say, "It killed me to see this happen" or "I could have killed him when he did that." In a story to express this feeling someone might get killed. Or we say "I felt weird." In a story an odd scene might convey a weird feeling. In your life you may or may not use this imaginative capacity. But it is there, in your dreams! It is a rich and good aspect of all humans.

Stories are a basic human dimension. During two out of every twenty-four hours human beings makes stories. Everyone dreams more than an hour *every* night. Research has shown that.

At first you might be obtuse and miss how stories represent something. But, you can be sure that your wider you is good at it, since you dream every night! You have this understanding of such stories, and you can get it consciously too. It won't take long, if you lovingly examine your dreams.

Let us go into detail.

Stories have a certain structure. *They go on in time.* Sequencing is important. *First* something happens, *then* something further, and only then the end.

It matters what comes first in the dream and what comes later.

If you don't remember the order, don't arrange the events artificially! Just note that you don't recall the order.

Suppose I dream of something nice and something scary. Which came first? Suppose first it was O.K., and then something scary came. That is very different from dreaming something scary which then came out all right. The first story says that something seemingly O.K. may turn scary, and we don't know how it might end. The second story says that something which seems scary turns out O.K.

Example: Armaments on the First Floor Dream

I entered a strange modern building. They were making armaments in the lobby, I think. There were guards and you could only go as far as the lobby. Somehow I got past the guards and into the elevator. Upstairs there was a large room, and some woman was pushing her way through an invisible barrier, like a membrane or rubber or something, but invisible. Then she got through and a man came from the other side and they danced a beautiful ballet.

Here the order of the events is important. First there are barriers, then she gets past them and the result is a beautiful dance, and togetherness. According to the dream, some barrier is not as bad as the person thinks. *First* it is scary, *then* something beautiful happens on the other side. The dream says that she gets across.

Many dreams end without resolution. One can say that we don't know yet, if the situation will resolve itself or not.

If the dream ends badly—and very many do—this indicates what the body envisions from the present constellation. The story is not a prediction. We don't *know* that the dreamer of the ballet dream *will* get across her barrier. All we know is that the body can already envision what that would be like. It is possible to get across.

Suppose I dreamed something like that in the opposite order. If the dream envisions my failure, I would look to see how and why I failed to get across. I would also look especially carefully at what happened just before I failed.

Example: Dirty Comb Dream

They said some little boy was sick. He was in the house and I was outside with Janet. They asked me to come and help. I gave them my comb and told them to take it to the boy. Later he died but they said it wasn't my fault.

I would summarize the story as: First the boy is sick and I'm asked to come and help. Then I send my comb. *Then* the boy dies. So the boy dies after I didn't go and sent my comb instead?

Now what is a comb to me? And what is the quality of sending it, since after that the boy dies? And I do this instead of going myself. What was my feel-quality in not going? Avoiding trouble, backing out, sort of, not coming to grips? Sort of. Well O.K., *that* quality, whatever it's called. And *that* quality leads to the boy's death. It's not a prediction of what will happen. Rather, it pictures what happens when I am avoidant in *that* way. The dream can help me tackle that way of being, so I can see what is in it, and change it.

Notice how we get to those helpful one-sentence summaries of dream-stories. We use "first there is this, then there is this." Fill the dream events into that formula. (Try including what you do, or don't do, as an event.)

If a dream has many events, there will be several versions. But even for just two events, there are different possible phrasings. I don't know in advance what they might say. I fill in this or that, and then I have a sentence with surprising implications. I try these out, one after the other, 'til something pops.

Let me do that with the example we just had, Armaments on the First Floor.

"First there is an uncrossable barrier. When I get across there's a man-woman ballet." Does that mean anything? With this summary you might stumble on a barrier specifically against man-woman combinations. Perhaps that lets something pop in. Perhaps not.

"First it seems to be about making guns, or something dangerous. Then there is a dance." The way this summary turns out, it might touch some anger or explosiveness (which might not be as bad as it seems).

"First I am down on the ground, and there are guards, then I get by them and go up." This might help find something guarded on the down-to-earth level.

"First I push against something I can't see, then there are two of us dancing." This emphasizes something I can feel in the way, but can't see.

Since I don't know what my dream means, I want to try several of these versons, until something moves in me.

QUESTION #6: CHARACTERS?

Take the unknown person in your dream. Or, if you know them all, take the most important. (Or take them up in turn.)
What does this person remind you of? What physical feel-qual-

ity does this person in the dream give you?
    Even a person whom you didn't see clearly may give you a
bodily sensed quality.
    With familiar people: Did the person look as usual?

If the unknown lady in the dream reminds you of your mother, she
includes some of your mother. But don't say, "She stands for my
mother." Why did the dream invent this unknown character? Your body
knows how to dream your mother and could easily have done that. You
have probably dreamed of your mother at some time. This unknown
character is not just your mother, though she may include some dimension of your mother. Who or what else does she remind you of?
    Familiar people sometimes look odd in a dream, because they are
combined with someone else. For example, "I dreamed of my mother,
but she was sort of fat." Here someone else is mixed together with
mother. Ask yourself who is fat, like that? (Also, what's the feel quality
of *this* fat?) Check if the familiar people looked unusual.
    But suppose you simply dreamed of your mother. The dream prob-
ably says something about your relationship with her. With Question #6
you see what comes if you take known dream-people as the real people
they are.

**Questions #4, #5, and #6 can be remembered together as Place,
Story, and Characters.**

QUESTION #7: WHAT PART OF YOU IS THAT?

    According to some theories, the other people in your dreams
are parts of you. We aren't sure that's true, but try it out:
    What feel-quality does this person give you? What sense
comes in your body? You needn't name it, just have it.
    If no quality comes, ask yourself: What is one adjective I could
use for that person?
    Now think of that adjective or feel-quality as a part of you.
    If *that* is a part of you, what part would that be?
    You may or may not like this part of you, or know much about
it. But let it be here for the moment, anyway.
    Does the dream make sense, if you take it as a story about
how you relate to that part of you?

    Example: Birthday Present Dream
    The others in the club asked me to let Bill sleep with my wife.

It was supposed to be a birthday present for Bill. I didn't like the idea, and I said she wouldn't do it anyway. In that case, they said Bill could sleep with my Aunt Beth.

Associations: "That dream is really crazy. I wouldn't let them ask me something like that. I don't know what club this is. O.K., what's Bill like? Bill always does only the part of the job he likes. He is unscrupulous and imposes on everybody. Hmm...that part of me? Well, yes (laugh). But I don't like that. I'm glad I'm not like Bill. But, umm, sure, there is that part of me. Get what I want. I'd run over everybody. I don't let it come up much, even inside."

Now he fills that into the dream: "She should sleep with *that* part of me? Hmm. For a birthday present? Not a bad idea.

"And, if she won't do it, then Aunt Beth? Oh, yea, Aunt Beth gave me lots of loving attention like my mother never did. So, hmm. Give that part of me lots of loving attention? Could I love that part of me? Hmm."

In Question #7 you try out considering the people as parts of you. Is the difference between Questions #6 and #7 clear to you? We don't decide if that is part of you, we try it that way.

Take especially an *unknown* person in your dream. After all, that person exists in no other way than as a part of you.

But how you feel the familiar real people can *also* be a part of you.

Ask: What is the outstanding quality of that person?

Suppose you dreamed of your friend Sharon. What is Sharon like? Get an adjective, let's say "forward" or "seductive." Or a longer description. "She has no trouble finding men." "She's easy-going about sex and expresses her feelings to anybody."

Now, if *that* (so named, or so felt) were part of you, what part would that be?

At this point you may find that you think you don't have a part like that. Sharon is your very opposite. You're not like that and you're glad. Fine. But since your conscious self excludes it, it is likely to be "a part" cut away from you and put where you don't see it.

When you do sense this part of you, fill it into the story. How does that part act, and how do you react to what it does?

Filling that in, what does the dream say *your* Sharon part does? And, according to the dream, how do you relate to your Sharon part? In the dream Sharon cuddles up to some guy and you are shocked and leave. Is that how you treat your own Sharon part? It shocks you and you leave? Does something stir in relation to that?

Even if the figure wasn't seen clearly in the dream, was the character tall, short, thin? How dressed? Even totally vague figures carry some feel-quality. Can we give it an adjective? Or we can call it *"that quality."*

Fill *that* into the story. What would the dream mean if the story is about how that part of you acts, and how you treat it?

Of course, we don't know that dream-characters are parts of you. It's likely though, since your body made them up. But it isn't anything we want to force on ourselves. We ask rather whether the dream makes sense, if you take it as a story about how you relate to that part of yourself.

An interpretation may pop, when you take the other persons in the dream as parts of you. Your whole interpretive set changes.

Example: Disheveled Man Dream
There was this very disheveled, downtrodden man living upstairs like a recluse in this old, broken-down house.

She said: "That's Gerry" [her husband]. "Sometimes I think of him like that."

But then comes Question #7: Is there a part of me, like that? It would be a masculine part. What is so-called "masculine?" The part of me that takes actions and fights for things, takes care of business..... Oh ..... yeah ..... I know that part of me is not in good shape. Hmm, so it lives like a recluse, by itself. Hmm. I'm giving it no attention, no company. It's downtrodden, hmm. I don't give it much respect in me. Hmm. And now I will fill that into the rest of the dream, to see what the dream-story says about it and about me.

Another example: Rocket Dream
My father is in a rocket that's about to be shot to outer space with some other people. He tells me to light a long-lasting bonfire in an empty lot, so he could see it for a long while as they get farther and farther away. Then he roughly shoves my hand off the curtain on the window so I cannot see him any more.

"My father died years ago. What part of me is like my father, or still connected to him? Hmm. ..... Now the story: it says that part of me is leaving forever? Hmm ..... Yes, I've been getting more and more free of his values and attitudes. I know that."

CONTROL, Part 1: "The opposite would be to hang on to it, or let it hang on. Hmm. Well, don't adopt the opposite, that isn't it either. Keep it open."

Now, CONTROL, Part 2: "What comes in there, in my body, if my father leaves for good? ..... [focusing] ..... Hmm.. There's, umm, that feeling of, 'Oh, no, don't let go yet'—What is that? I'm not willing to let him go, yet, I guess. ..... Oh, he isn't willing to let go of me yet. Yea. Build a long-lasting fire ..... feels like that, yes. ..... Oh, sure, I'm afraid he's mad at me, yes. That way he closed the window shade, that feels like he might be mad at me. Yes. That's an old, old childhood feeling, too! Whew."

QUESTION #8: BE THAT PERSON?

Stand up or sit forward on the edge of the chair. *Loosen your body.* Now imagine that you are preparing to act in a play. The play is tomorrow. Now you are just getting ready, feeling yourself into the role. You are going to play that character from the dream. *Let the feel-quality of being that person come in your body.*

You can actually do this now, or just imagine it, but *be sure to do it in your body.*

How would you walk on stage? With a stomp, or stiffly, or how? How would you stand or sit? How would your shoulders be? Don't decide. Let your body do it of its own accord.

Exaggerate it. Let's say it's a ham play. Overdo it so that the audience would laugh.

What comes to you to say or to do? Don't make it up. Wait and see what words or moves come from the body-feel.

See if you can take that with you. If you think of that character's image again, does the quality come again in your body?

These questions can be applied to anything in a dream, not only to people. As in Charades, one can say, "Be that wall" or any object from the dream. Wait and sense what comes in your body. (For example, you are playing the wall. You stand. Suddenly it comes to you to stretch out your arm with a stiff blocking motion, and you say, "Halt!")

You can also act your own usual way of being, as you were in the dream. Exaggerate it, see what it is when you let it be even more so. [See Mark's Dream, Ch. 9.]

In my classes we stand up, loosen our bodies, and use this question without visible acting. If you were observing, you would only see us standing silently. Soon you would hear exclamations and laughter, as something comes to most of the class. Surprise on many faces is all you could see. And, in class most people don't say what came.

It is important to loosen the body—at least don't sit in the same position you were sitting without moving a little. Let go of the body-set you had, so a new one can form. Then *wait.* Let it come in your body.

The idea is *not* to write a play, but to let the dream figure *come in your body*. You are sensing your way into the part.

If you want to get up and act it out, that's best. But you can stay seated and sense what comes in your body to act this role.

Mere description is not enough. I interrupt you if you say, "I know how I would act this person, I would...." I say, "Don't tell me. Let it come in your body."

If words or moves come suddenly, without your first having a felt sense, find the felt sense right afterwards. *Sense the source of those spontaneous words and acts.* For example, suppose tears come. Let your attention go to the source of the tears, where something cries inside you.

Or suppose you found yourself saying: "Enough, I've had it with you, cut that out! Sense now, in your body, that new solidity, that sense of insistence—*that* body-sense." (You don't need words describing it.)

Overact it. Exaggerate it until it is funny. For example, let us say you are usually very considerate and sensitive. You dream of a callous boor. Don't act just a little callous. Let your body "ham it up" as you would in a theater for kids. What would your body do for a *huge, joyous callousness?* Perhaps your body spreads the arms and legs all over the space and knocks into everybody. Or perhaps your nose points into the air and your arm waves everybody off with an exaggerated gesture of dismissal.

What interprets the dream is the physical sense of a new way of being, an inward shift, the new energy-quality in your body. You sense directly what it would be like to live more *that* way.

You may find various bodily sensations and tensions. If they are there, fine. But attend in the middle of your body, that is where a felt sense comes.

As I said earlier, if you flatly refuse to "be" that person, and you say, "Not in a million years, not that one," please be interested in that intense feeling. What is that strong resistance? It is interesting, is it not? Focus on that feeling for a little while, and be very understanding and gentle with it. It will tell you what it is, not in one step, but over several little steps.

In working with others you might have to struggle a little, explain the question better, not be deterred by an initial unwillingness. Sometimes it helps if you imagine how you would act the character for a moment, and then ask the dreamer in what way that's wrong. The dreamer then often has a very instant sense of what would be right. Of course, you wouldn't get the whole process stuck by insisting that the person do Question #8. No single question needs to be used. Each person must sense inside what is or is not helpful. But don't accept mere stage fright or embarrassment; point out that it can be done privately and inwardly. People don't understand this question at first, if they have never done it.

But if actually doing this question does not feel good in your body, then, of course, stop. That is an overarching principle about following anyone's instructions with any human process: How it actually feels in you must be the ultimate guide.

Is this question really safe? Suppose you get a flash of anger down in you. How do you know it's safe to feel that anger? Some self-assertive anger is a perfectly good thing and part of a healthy person. If it has been shunted aside for years, it might seem very strong and violent. *If* you do, in fact, sometimes physically attack people with uncontrolled violence, then don't do this question. But if this is true of you, you probably don't dream violent characters as not-you. But most people haven't even kicked a wall for years.

You may sense your anger as negative, resentful, old, and corroded, when it comes. Take it as it comes, but expect it to turn into healthy anger or a sense of strength. Don't design or figure out how it ought to be. Let it come as it is. It may change quickly, or need a little time. Welcome the energy so it does not have to stay stuck.

What is split off, *not* felt, remains the same. When it is felt, it changes. Most people don't know this! They think that by *not* permitting the feeling of their negative ways they make themselves good. On the contrary, that keeps these negatives static, the same from year to year. A few moments of feeling it in your body allows it to change.

If there is in you something bad, sick, or unsound, let it inwardly be and breathe. That's the only way it can evolve and change into the form it needs.

One type of figure you find in dreams is what Jung named "the shadow." This is an opposite of your usual personality. For example, if you are a peaceable person, violent figures are like that for you. Since it is your opposite, you are likely to be repelled by it. But your rejection can be more subtle. You might say this figure is dull, not significant, not worth attention.

In my own dreams I long missed the significance of some of the characters. I didn't want to try out "being" them because they seemed "boring." "That's interesting, isn't it?" I find myself writing next. I am a person who cares a lot about what is interesting. I like to explore, to experiment, to see new things. I enjoy thinking. I am an intellectual. I am a college professor, a writer, a therapist, above all, a philosopher. What do you suppose I would reject most? Something "boring."

For many years my dreams had cab drivers, businessmen in dull pinstripe suits, farmers. Especially cab drivers! The cab driver was often rude. *He* would not stop to let me out where I wanted to go. He decided where I should go. One farmer in my dream had oil on his property. What is his outstanding quality? "Very boring and ordinary," I said at first. But a farmer with oil on his property isn't ordinary!

And those businessmen? One major growth direction in my life soon showed up: becoming a little more effective in action, in arrangements, in publicizing, in getting my work out. For years I had not been getting my work all the way out—effectively, so it would reach people. To learn that took some doing! Anyone who knows me knows the change it was for me. It took time. At first these actions made me feel sick! After a while I began to laugh and brag that I was "becoming a businessman."

That was not just learning a new competence. It balanced my personality. It felt like a second leg was added, as if I had had only one before that. It was part of a wider change in my way of being alive. But at first the businessmen in my dreams seemed boring and trivial to me.

But I will never become the opposite type of person. This change and development of my personality comes by just adding a little bit of the opposite, and at that in my own way. If you are very sedentary, a little bit of exercise can make a very great difference. But don't worry, you will not become a professional athlete because of it. About my being good at business, I joke and tell people: "When I'm eighty, I'll get to the point where I'm merely below average."

If you dream of someone you can't stand, don't be afraid you'll really become like that person. You couldn't. More *of you* will come through if you try out "being" that person. The dream image isn't really that "so and so." *It is your body's own.*

You can never lose your main developed way. Now, with your same body, be the other way.

Question #8 is the only method I know by which one can immediately sense "the other side." Especially if one's usual way is always nice, easly oppressed and depressed, there is great value in being the mean oppressor for a few minutes.

This role reversal is fascinating. Oppression and meanness are familiar to you, of course, but only as coming at you. Now this dream figure from your body lets you take the other role. In real life you will not do that, probably quite rightly not. But in your body, for a minute, do it. Then your body will make something new.

Exaggerate it so much that you laugh. Would you come on stage with a devil's costume? Would you like claws? Spew flames? Make monster noises? If not like that, how?

Of course you may also know that part of you quite well. Even so, being that way more fully and with your whole body might change its split-off form.

Or: Let the dream story tell you how it acts, and you toward it. Then keep your mind open for an as yet undefined new way you might act toward it. Think of various possibilities. Then imagine the character and let your body react spontaneously.

Another way exists, if you don't wish to be that character. You can work at confronting it instead, and standing your ground with it.

For example: Nazi Dream

The Nazis had taken over. We could be shot any time, and it was certain that we would be, sooner or later. I went through some room and wasn't shot yet, but it was no use fighting back or hiding.

"I refuse to *be* a Nazi. But sure, I could use more fighting energy than I showed in the dream. Hmm..... Feels like it's no use fighting, I'd only get killed. Hmm..... Seems like I don't want to confront, engage, stand my ground. I want to have nothing to do with the whole thing. Nothing. Well, hmm..... Yes. I can sense something coming more alive, if I assume I'm going to stand my ground, meet them some way. Hmm..... Right! Why should I avoid the damn bastards!

"Well, that's a new energy. Why avoid *anything,* damn it!"

Here he did not assume the role of the Nazi, but in being more confronting and challenging in relation to the Nazi, his energy came.

In general, if it feels quite wrong to *be* that character, try relating to the character in some way that is new for you.

One can also ask:

If this were a real situation, what would you do?

"With the Nazi? I think in that situation I wouldn't know what else to do, than in the dream."

Well, what else might one do?

Or, with the American Perfectionist dream (Chapter 5): If this were a real situation and some man was carrying everything you owned out of your house, what would you do?

Question #8 comprises both your being that person and how you might act toward that person. You might get a step on either side.

QUESTION #9: CAN THE DREAM CONTINUE?

Vividly visualize the end, or any one important scene of the dream. Feel it again. When it comes back as fully as possible, just watch it and wait for something further to happen.

Wait for it, don't invent anything.

Later: What impulse do you have, if any, to do something back at the image once it has done something of its own accord?

These three questions are from Jung and Perls. I have made the role of the body specific.

One of the three is often enough. You would not usually need all three at once. You can use the other two later, if you need them.

Revisualize the end, or any important bit of the dream. Then just watch it. Expect something to happen.

When it does, ask yourself: What action-impulse do you have, now? What would you do back at the image, now that it has done that? Wait, let something come from your body.

(part of longer dream:) ....then she made this nasty comment (which is what she often does) and I just left her there and went on down the street.

I revisualized her making the comment, and let it continue from there: She grabbed me around the chest and pulled me down. I had a sinking feeling, which made me unhappy. I thought, yes, she would really pull me down if she could.

Now, what do I do in return?... I waited. Then:

Suddenly I got on top of her and beat her, and then I took her by both wrists and dragged her off!

When completing a dream image, let it go as far as it will, until it feels complete, and won't do more (see Malamud 1979).

From focusing we have learned that these dream-continuations can come from sensing in the body. *Let it well up* from attending *in the body;* don't invent it. In the above example the person was not asking himself to do anything. His action came of its own accord.

Questions #7, #8, and #9 can be remembered as three ways to work further with the characters.

QUESTION #10 about symbols was discussed separately in Chapter 12.

QUESTION #11: BODY ANALOGY?

> Something in a dream may be an analogy for the body. For example, a long object may be a penis, a purse may stand for a vagina. The car may be your sexual activity. A house may be your body.
> Does this fit? The attic or other high place can mean thought, being in your head, far from feelings.
> Downstairs, ground level, can mean feelings, being in your body lower down, grounded.
> The basement, underground, or underwater can mean the unconscious, or what is not visible.
> Odd-looking machines and diagrams often make sense if viewed as body analogies.

Example: Elevator Dream
I was going up in an elevator. As it got very high, the whole thing became very shaky and wobbled. I got out on the twenty-fifth floor. But I couldn't get back down; the elevator wouldn't go down. . . [dream continues].

Now you ask yourself: "What would it mean if being up high meant being in your head, and going down meant being lower in my body?... Can I sense how coming down would be, in my body? ... Something's in the way of coming down! I have to stay with this a little while."

Example: Ice on the Motor Dream
I owned a motorcycle. (I've always wanted one but women aren't supposed to.) It was standing, or rather, leaning against the garage wall. There was ice on the motor and on the back wheel.

"Well, if the motor is frozen, it won't start. My wanting a motorcycle is on ice, I guess. Let me feel that in my body, my wanting a motorcycle. ..... Oh!, sure! My sexual desire is on ice, too. Ice is like an anesthetic. I don't feel the desire. ..... But I could."

In this example the motorcycle is analogous to the body. What part of the body corresponds to the motor and the rear wheel?

QUESTION #12: COUNTERFACTUAL?

> What in the dream is specifically different from the actual situation?
> Exactly what has the dream changed?

Example: Wall Dream
A wall (which isn't really there) ran the whole length of my apartment, dividing it in two long halves.

If the dream went out of its way to change the situation in just certain respects, ask: Why would it make just these changes?

Or: Does the dream picture something different in value, opposite from how you evaluate it in waking life? Does someone you think of as stupid appear unusually large and impressive in the dream? Is someone pictured small, silly, or disheveled whom you in fact admire? Is something you consider worthless represented as hauntingly beautiful? See if the dream "corrects" your waking attitude. If so, try out a more moderate attitude in between.

Example: Large Father Dream
In the dream, my father came to visit, but he was huge. Linda and I just came up to his boots. And our house was tiny.

Question: "Could it mean something, if I tried out saying that he is much more important to me than I tell myself? Let me be quiet and see if anything comes to me."

Example: Dizzy Librarian Dream
I was returning books to the library. The woman behind the counter was a dizzy dame, sort of. She counted the books but then she wrote down a different number than she said. She told me various rules and complicated procedures for returning the books. I said I was returning them, that's all, and I left.

"Who does the dizzy dame remind me of? Sandy, the way she looked. But Sandy is one of the smartest people I know in this whole world!"

Maybe you overestimate Sandy in some way?

Try it in your body:

"Hmm.... I can feel that I *want* to keep thinking she's so very smart.... What is that sense of wanting to think that?"

Question #12 is not an oracle saying you should or should not think more or less highly about that person or thing. Rather, *it leads to a question you might not otherwise ask yourself and sense.*

For example, take the dream about the large father. Some investigators would say it shows that the father means too much to the person already. Others would say the dreamer needs to correct a view of the father that is too small. The experts can't agree, so your body must decide.

Try it out both ways. Perhaps you know your father is too important to you. But he is getting old. Perhaps you ought to be see him or do more for him, since you are going to feel his death intensely. Who knows?

Another example: Huge Back Dream
I was with this woman on a bed and there were some other men there, not just me. Then she told them to leave so we could be alone. I saw that they were teen-agers, really, but they were very big, one had a huge back, I saw as they left. Then we were alone and I think we made out.

Does it make sense to ask about some teen-age aspect of you? Do you think of it as very important or as not important?

Does the huge back mean this aspect is larger than you had thought? Or perhaps the image shows more of how large it is. Only you can decide. The story here (Question #5) says that when the teen-agers leave, you get to make love. Does that open up something?

What opens newly inside you can tell you. Otherwise, there are only the differing guesses.

Example: Subway Dream
I am desperately trying to find the subway. I ask some guys on the street. They point and say, "The subway is right over there."
I see a place with two entrances, one is the subway, the other is something else, and someone is shooting at me from there. I run up the subway steps, the steps actually went to an elevated platform. But in the dream I thought of it as a subway. A train comes and stops. That's all. Station closed. I go back downstairs and see someone with a gun. I try to duck but get shot.

There is a lot to explore here, but the counterfactual is striking. From the street he ran *up* the subway steps.

Here are some questions to ask: (Using his first answers, one would go on in various ways, of course.)

What could it mean that you go up instead of down?

What is a subway? What does a subway do? Suppose he answers: "It gets one to a different place fast, deep under the ground." Filling that into the dream leads to the next question.

What could this mean: you think you're moving in a fast, deep way, but actually you're going up into your thoughts?

Does this fit anything you know? You escape some way, and then when you come back, the problem gets you just the same?

What do you do with anger? Does it fit to say that you sometimes think you've coped with it when perhaps you haven't?

In general, what is contrary to fact in dreams is worth asking about.

Questions #10, #11, and #12 are three decodings: Symbols, Body Analogy, and Counterfactual.

QUESTION #13: CHILDHOOD?

> What childhood memory might come in relation to the dream?
> If you think of your childhood, what comes?
> In your childhood, what had this feel-quality from the dream?
> What went on in your life at that time? What was it like for you?

Example: Rickety Stairs Dream

It was very nice with large rooms and lovely woodwork. The stairs near the top were very rickety. They sort of wobbled.

Association: "When I was little I had an attic that had rickety stairs like that. You had to put your foot down very carefully and hang on to something while you did it."

Now the childhood memory leads her to what was going on for her at that time. (Or you would ask yourself: What went on for me then?)

"I used to go up into that attic and sit there for hours. It would comfort me, umm .... I remember getting beaten a lot, in that time. I've always remembered that, but, umm ... [takes a breath].... In the years since then, I have realized it was a lot worse than I let myself believe then. I've remembered it but I've stayed away from it. I said well, that happens in most families. But... [breathes]... I can touch that now, just a little bit, in me. It felt good to do that, now. It has been pushed aside for such a long time. I, umm, I don't want too much of it all at once."

As Freud said, just about everyone has to recall childhood events and sense how they are, inside. Then they change somewhat. One can then overcome certain limitations one could not overcome before.

The *interpretation* of a dream may depend on your doing some of that, otherwise you would have no interpretation, only guesses.

With this dream someone might have guessed: Upstairs and downstairs could represent the body. The connection is rickety, so the person has some access to deeper, or bodily, or grounded ways, but it's rickety and uneasy. Something remains to be worked out. Someone might have guessed also: It's probably something from childhood (since it is almost universal for humans that our troubles begin then). Someone might have guessed also: Probably certain childhood events haven't been fully attended to, so they're in the way of free and solid access. So often we stay away from one or two things only, but avoiding these blocks up one's whole access to one's body and to one's wholeness.

But this would have been mere generalities. One could perhaps say this of every single human being. Compare these thin generalities with the actual association and the deeper opening it immediately brings her. Also, these generalities were only only one set of guesses. Other equally good guesses would have been made as well. Then we would have no interpretation, only conflicting hypotheses.

An actual interpretation is usually the same thing as the actual bodily step. Here it is the actual memory, the actual direct sense of what is to be done with it, and the actual doing of that.

Opening such a dream's meaning is the same thing as opening and sensing that childhood memory.

Here is why you might want to do that:

A dream is about your present life and growth, not only about your childhood. What the memory brings is probably relevant today. Don't get stuck with: "Yes, that's how it was. I never got over that they didn't love me. . ." or whatever the childhood memory brings. Right now, your ways of living and your attitudes involve what the childhood memory expresses. How you live now is open. How you live now can change how your childhood is in you, and what it does to you.

People are not mathematical sums of what happened to them.

However, we often live in ways that repeat our childhood themes. We set up situation after situation so the same thing happens. But the organism is made to live well, and as a whole. The repetitions are not only bad. They are also beginnings of overcoming what maimed and cut you in childhood. The body begins again and again to overcome it. The issue is always there again. But the direction of healing is also indicated, if you let your body give you that direction.

How can the body do that? It is like when you hold your breath: your body wants to exhale. When you sit cramped for ten minutes, it wants to stand up. When you hold anger in, the body wants to express it. When you suppress sexuality, the body wants it. When you are always nice and put yourself last, the body produces a dream-mugger who puts himself first. And so on. The childhood memory is therefore not just something to deplore. It is an issue that your body never stops trying to move beyond.

So when such a memory comes, sense which way would be more life and fresh air. But you do have to feel the old feelings that emerge from the memory. In my example, you do have to have the cramped feeling if you are to sense your body's direction and desire to stand up from being cramped. So don't push the old feeling away and try to substitute something better. The direction will be in the bad feeling. When that comes, mark it and keep it so you can feel the cramped feeling plus the standing-up feeling, over and over.

Sometimes the life-direction does not come so quickly. Many people have found it vitally helpful to just tolerate feeling how it was, what happened, what it felt like. What we could not stand as children gets shut away at the time. Then it helps just to let it out, and let it breathe.

You gingerly touch that old hurt or fright, just a little, many times, over and over. After a while the healing appears in it.

QUESTION #14: PERSONAL GROWTH?

> How are you developing, or trying to develop?
> What do you struggle with or wish you could be or do?
> In what way are you a one-sided, not a well-rounded, person?
> Could the dream or the characters in it represent what you still need to develop? Suppose the dream were a story about that? What might it mean?

Recall various areas of your life. A dream is likely to be about the edges, the limitations, which your body struggles to overcome.

Some people never think of these; some think of them all the time.

Where is your life hung up? What would you like to do, how would you like to be? What would you do if you were not too scared? What are you resigned about? Why is life gray? What are the borders and edges of your life?

If you are fairly satisfied with yourself, that's good. It need not be an illusion. Even so, vast development is possible for any person; it is more exciting than traveling, more interesting than way-out adventures. If you don't *need* to change and grow, you still *want* to.

But you might answer: "What I think of is a better job, and I wish I could get my husband to act better—but these things depend on other people. How can I find 'edges' of my person, like you mean?" These externals can lead you to your edges: What happens to you *inside* in relation to these things? What, in you, can't stand this job, and what in you has given up on a new job? What kind of feelings, fears, and struggles come when you think of trying? Where does it get you, inside, how your husband acts? What in you is stirred up? That way, soon, you will find your own edges. It may help with the external situation too, after you grow a few steps inside. You may get stronger and clearer so that you can deal with the other people better.

We fail at many things for years. They need us to grow *as a whole*. Instead, we keep trying to fix only the situation. Often there is no way. The situation isn't our fault, and yet: The constellation I am fails over and over at this type of situation. A more global change may be needed. I might have to get less interested in this one aim and more interested *in myself*, the kind of person I am, my inward growth and being. Where is that cramped? Where is that limited? In what ways have I given up on myself long ago and could now begin, after all, to grow?

You might say: "I'm too old. If I now became able at what I couldn't be before, what good would it do? I couldn't get what I missed when I was young." That might be true, you might no longer be able to *get* what you missed. But you can still get your development, get to *be*.

Many people do say: "Life isn't all about getting" and that's true. But people say this as a cover for not developing. They say, "I missed a lot that I would have gotten if I had been different. But it's too late to change myself now. Life isn't about getting, anyway." Such a person knows truly that life is not about how much you can get and consume. Yet there may be a dull, overly resigned quality of giving up. That is the quality of *missed development of the human essence*. It is not about getting something.

You can *now* move to develop! That might not bring what you missed, but the dull, closed giving up will be replaced by new energy. The development (and even just the very move toward it) expands the person.

When Aunt Mitz was seventy years old, she realized one day with great suddenness that she had lived her whole life for other people and proper appearances. Somehow instead of depressing her, it gave her a new life. She said, "Too bad it's so late, but now I'm free." Then she told her husband, "I'm traveling around the world. If you want, you can come with me." She sold her things and went. She had a few years of *being* that free way.

A lot of the bad feeling of what one missed is the fact that one is still the same. One would miss it all over again! With hindsight one could have avoided the losses in those old situations. But in analagous situations today, one still behaves the same way! When that changes, the losses are far easier to stand.

Even if one cannot immediately be a new way, just turning to struggle with one's limits is energy-giving. There is fresh air in the challenge. How much one changes is a question of results, success. It is a kind of "getting." But regardless of results and successes, turning in a growth-direction is a good way of being alive.

Old people say it's too late for them. But they tell young people: "This is the time you should be enjoying life. That's important." It's so "important" that it's paralyzing. It might be better to say, "You don't have to enjoy life."

One wants freedom, play, and love of life for its own sake. Development is for its own sake, for its freed energy-thrust and uncramping. That bodily quality is lost if one falls too hard for pressure and threat. One gets trapped into working only on performance abilities, and then, tensely, fails at those. A free person puts the human essence well above the success values. You care about the results, sure. But, whatever the results, moving into a growth-direction is worth doing in itself.

Dreams can bring the directions that actually feel this way together with the energy-shifting steps that begin to make them real.

If you don't have a sense of your next development (also with any insoluble problem), open a little space inside yourself for steps to come. You do it this way: Although you cannot imagine a possible step, attend to the dull, flat, or hurt sense in your body as if a little step might come. Then, if nothing comes, keep the asking, there. Let the asking make a "there." If that space is empty just now, that's O.K. Keep that space open. Check back with it often. Expect a little step to come into it after a while, from a dream or in some other way.

Then, when you have a dream, you can ask this question: Does something from the dream relate itself to that asking-space I'm keeping, there?

QUESTION #15: SEXUALITY?

> Try the dream out as a story about whatever you are currently doing or feeling about sexuality.
> Or: If it were a story about your ways of being sexual, what would it be saying?

Freud held that every human experience is in some way sexual. He thought of life-energy as inherently sexual.

Freud showed that there is often an analogy between how we act sexually and other behaviors of ours. This is true. You are the same person, the same constellation, whether making love or doing something else. If I love to plan projects but never do any of them, you won't be surprised if I am better at sexual foreplay than the rest of it. On the other hand, if I am externally oriented and have a brass-tacks attitude toward everything, my wife is likely to say, "All he cares about is the aim." If I am afraid of new situations, I might be upset if she wants to try new ways of making love with me. And so on.

These examples have been overly simple. If you examine your feelings in sexuality you will find them complex. They will manifest some of the same complexities that you also have in other contexts.

Freud would have said that our problems in the other contexts are basically sexual problems. We need not accept or reject that. We can try it out in both directions. Sex and anything else can be analogies for each other.

In the dream something sexual can express a way you are that matters most in other contexts.

Example: Drunk Woman Dream

I am looking right at a woman across the way who has taken her clothes off. She is drunk, and I feel a little sheepish about taking advantage of her by looking at her. I know tomorrow she will feel bad about doing this now.

Associations: "I do have a voyeuristic streak. I like to look at naked women. But I already knew that."

What in your life is like that? You do it, but you feel sheepish?

"Aha! A breakthrough. I know what that is! [deep breath] Yeah, it's time I tackle that."

Is whatever that is, about sex?

"No, it isn't. It's about getting into things but not all the way, sort of half-way, and then feeling that sheepish way about dropping out of them. It's about a lot of things, one especially."

Here it doesn't matter whether a sexual problem manifests in other areas, or whether it is a general problem expressed in a sexual story. The same constellation manifests in both places. Just now this sexual dream led to a step that is more important in other areas. Conversely, a dream may not be overtly sexual and yet the breakthrough may come the moment you think of it sexually.

How might it be a story about you and sexuality?

QUESTION #16: SPIRITUALITY?

What creative or spiritual potential of yours might the dream be about?

Are there dimensions of being human in the dream that you don't take much account of in your life?

Thief in a Mansion Dream
This huge mansion was full of gold and antiques. I was a thief. I went in and stole the sheets from under the bedspreads. The bedspreads were gold. I left them slightly rumpled.

What would you say is the difference between sheets and bedspreads?

"Well, you need sheets, but bedspreads are just for decoration."

Do you mostly spend your life on what's needed, with little time for beauty?

"It's true I don't have much time for things like beauty, for myself."

What about spiritual things?

"Do you mean my faith? I gave that up when I was 22."

Well, what might come if you try saying: I've mostly used everything for work and needs. Does something in me want my life to be more than that?"

Let's take someone who is outwardly quite ordinary. Inwardly the person is aware of some odd experiences—everyone is. People are afraid to talk about these. Perhaps she is scared of going crazy, or having people call her crazy. She might be fighting suicide at times; many outwardly ordinary people are. Or perhaps she is just bored and going along with a vague sense that life should have been more. Perhaps not even that.

If you asked her: "Do you think some spiritual development might be possible for you?" she might wonder what you mean. She might think you could only mean orthodox religion.

Or if you asked, "Have you ever thought of being a poet?" she might laugh. If she does sometimes write poems, she would be embarrassed inside.

People often put spiritual and esthetic dimensions far away from themselves. And yet they are part of every person.

Dreams can ask you just this kind of question: Would you like some spiritual development? Might you become a poet? How about some esthetic experience; you haven't developed that. How about some of the mystery of the universe? See the ocean? The dream may present something with a vast glow, something *so-o-o* beautiful!

Don't miss it when a dream could let you sense a spiritual direction—especially if that is the furthest thing from your mind.

But suppose you have no way to think about spirituality? It hasn't ever made sense to you. Then just keep this dream's sense. Its symbols and images may say the direction better than words can.

But also, if you do have many concepts about spirituality, don't impose them on the dream. Let the dream take you further, where you have not yet thought. Let its own sense be here. You can conceptualize later.

If there is something hauntingly beautiful or impressive in your dream, just honor it, respect it, recall it, sense it with your body. More will come.

Whatever life is now, why run through the rest of it the same way? Why watch the movie to the end, if you could figure out what will happen? Do you feel you can figure out, write the rest of your life from here? Move into a new dimension! Among what is best in being human, what has been furthest from you? You need not understand it in advance. Let your dream hint you to it.

BIBLIOGRAPHY

Berry, P. 1974. An approach to the dream. *Spring:* 58–79.

Bonime, M. 1962. *The clinical use of dreams.* New York: Basic Books.

Boss, M. 1958. *The analysis of dreams.* A. J. Pomerans, trans. New York: Philosophical Library.

Epstein, G. N. 1981. *Waking dream therapy.* New York: Human Sciences Press.

Gendlin, E. T. 1962. *Experiencing and the creation of meaning.* New York: Free Press.

_____. 1967. Neurosis and human nature in the experiential method of thought. *Humanitas* 3:139–52.

_____. 1971. A phenomenology of emotions: Anger. In *Explorations in phenomenology,* D. Carr & E. Casey, eds. The Hague: Martinus Nijhoff.

_____. 1973. Experiential phenomenology. In *Phenomenology and the social sciences,* M. Nathanson, ed. Evanston: Northwestern University Press.

_____. 1977. Phenomenological concept vs. phenomenological method: A critique of Medard Boss. *Soundings* LX: 285-300.

_____. 1981. *Focusing.* New York: Bantam Books.

_____. 1982. Two phenomenologists do not disagree. In *Phenomenology, dialogues and bridges.* R. Bruzina & B. Wilshire, eds. Albany: State University of New York Press.

_____. 1984. The politics of giving therapy away. In *Teaching psychological skills: Models for giving therapy away,* D. Larson, ed. Monterey, Cal.: Brooks/Cole.

_____. 1986. Philosophical critique of the concept of narcissism. In *Modern pathologies of the self,* D. M. Levin, ed. New York: New York University Press.

_____ with Grindler, D., & McGuire, M. 1984. Imagery, body, and space. In *Imagination and healing,* A. A. Sheikh, ed. New York: Baywood.

Hendricks, M., & Cartwright, R. D. 1978. Experiencing level in dreams: An individual difference variable. *Psychotherapy: Theory, research and practice* 15:292–98.

Malamud, J. R. 1967. An experiential approach to understanding dreams. Unpublished paper, University of Chicago.

_____. 1979. The development of a training method for the cultivation of "lucid" awareness in fantasy, dreams, and waking life. Unpublished Ph.D. dissertation, New York University.

Mathieu-Coughlan, P., & Klein, M. H. 1984. Experiential psychotherapy: Key events in client-therapist interaction. In *Patterns of change,* L. N. Rice & L. S. Greenberger, eds. New York: Guilford Press.

Sherman, E. 1984. *Working with older persons.* Boston: Kluwer-Nijhoff.

Ullman, M. 1979. *Working with dreams.* New York: Delacorte Press.

Whitmont, E. C. 1978. Martha's dream. In *Dream interpretation: A comparative study,* J. Fosshage & C. Lowe, eds. New York: Spectrum Books.

Index to Dreams

For latest information on Focusing, send one stamped self-addressed envelope to E. T. Gendlin, Ph.D., Dept. of Behavioral Sciences, University of Chicago, 5848 S. University, Chicago, Ill. 60637.

Mr./Mrs./Miss _____

Address _____

City _____ State _____ Zip _____

← Index to Dreams